Tried and Tested Ways
to Reduce Your VAT Bill

THE COMPLEMENTARY WEBSITE

The http://books.indicator.co.uk website gives you instant access to all the ready-to-use documents, tools, policies, etc. that complement this publication.

Go to

http://books.indicator.co.uk

and enter your access code
ECX293

THE CD-ROM

Don't have access to the Internet?
Call Customer Services on 01233 653500 to request a CD-ROM.

Indicator Ltd has joined forces with FL Memo Ltd

Cover: ©iStockphoto.com

Second Edition - First Print - E02P1

ISBN 978-1-906892-60-9

Introduction

Tried and Tested Ways to Reduce Your VAT Bill

When VAT was introduced over 30 years ago it was described as a "simple purchase tax"; today it's anything but. The idea is that only the final purchaser of goods or services should pay VAT, but on the way from producer to retailer VAT has to be added and reclaimed at each stage. Get it wrong and you could end up footing the bill instead of your customer.

VAT is the one tax which applies to all businesses, meaning that the rules and regulations are numerous, and if you don't stick to them the VATman has a range of tough penalty measures to hit you with. However, it's often said that the more rules you make, the greater the number of loopholes there will be, but of course to make use of these you need to know where to look.

This book covers the ins-and-outs of VAT from the registration process, to filling in returns and all the way through to trading in the EU and beyond. Each topic is considered in a logical way making it easy to follow and includes many examples to show how the rules commonly apply in practice. You'll find plenty of useful tips on how to save VAT or just make dealing with the VATman easier. Plus, we've highlighted the traps which businesses often fall into.

Andrew Walls

November 2012

Table of contents

Chapter 1 - Registration

Chapter 2 - VAT liability

Chapter 3 - Special accounting schemes

Chapter 4 - Output tax - charging VAT

Chapter 5 - Input tax

Chapter 6 - Returns

Chapter 7 - Capital goods scheme

Chapter 8 - Partial exemption

Chapter 9 - Selling or buying a business as a going concern

Chapter 10 - Penalties

Chapter 11 - Schemes for promoting your business

Chapter 12 - VAT and your business premises

Chapter 13 - International trade

Chapter 14 - VAT special situations

Chapter 15 - Appendices

CHAPTER 1

Registration

1.1. DO YOU NEED TO REGISTER?

1.1.1. What is VAT registration?

The VAT register is just a list of businesses that have to submit VAT returns, and the act of registration is simply the process of adding a business to that list. But contrary to popular belief, not every business has to be registered.

Most businesses on the list are there because their turnover exceeds limits set by the government, others are on it because it suits them to be registered. However, many businesses spend a lot of time and effort trying to avoid registering altogether.

1.1.2. Who has to register?

The VAT registration limit is £77,000 until April 1 2013 at least. This limit is reviewed and usually increases in line with inflation each year. A person in business, such as a sole trader, partnership or company, is required to register when their taxable turnover exceeds the limit set under either one of two tests.

The historic turnover test

The person is required to monitor taxable turnover at the end of each month. If at that time cumulative taxable turnover in the last twelve months (or since commencement of trade, whichever is shorter) exceeds the limit, they are required to notify HMRC within 30 days. They will then be registered with effect from the start of the following month. For example, a business has cumulative turnover of £77,000 in the twelve months to December 31; it has until January 30 to notify HMRC and will be registered with effect from February 1. There's a small window of opportunity for planning here.

> **TIP**
>
> In the example above the business knows in January that it will have to charge and account for VAT from February 1. This means that it has the whole of January to make supplies without having to charge VAT. It can offer customers who can't reclaim VAT, to pay early and avoid the VAT charge. Consider an electrician working for private clients. If he can persuade them to pay before he registers, they'll avoid VAT which should keep them happy. The electrician is happy too as he's been paid early for his work.

The future turnover test

In addition to monitoring turnover at the end of each month for the purposes of the historic test, the business must also look forward. If there are reasonable grounds for believing that in the following 30 days alone its turnover will exceed the registration limit, it must notify the VATman. It has 30 days in which to do this.

The difference is that the date the VATman will register the business from will be the date that it was clear the turnover limit would be exceeded.

EXAMPLE

A business with a typical turnover of £8,000 per month receives a one-off order for £70,000 of goods on April 10 2013 and expects to deliver these to its customer in three weeks. The business has every expectation that the turnover limit will be exceeded in the next 30 days and has until May 10 to notify the VATman, who will then register the business with effect from April 10.

1.1.3. What is taxable turnover?

It's important to note that when looking at turnover for registration purposes you only consider taxable turnover. This means the value of supplies made by the business which would be subject to VAT at either the standard, reduced or zero rates (see Chapter 2).

Any supplies which would be exempt or outside the scope of VAT can be ignored, as can investment income. See Appendix 1 for examples of turnover or income that can be ignored for registration purposes. This can result in businesses not being required to register for VAT despite generating income way over the turnover limit.

1.1.4. Who's responsible for registering?

VAT registration applies to a person rather than the business. Thus, a sole trader with different businesses must add the turnover from each to assess whether they need to be registered.

EXAMPLE

Donald Derby runs a management consultancy practice turning over £70,000 per annum. He is also a keen gardener and opens his garden to the public at weekends in the summer. From this he generates a further £8,000. His total turnover is £78,000 and he is required to register for VAT.

1.1.5.   Is being VAT registered a good or a bad thing?

There's no simple answer to this question but the following table sets out some of the factors to bear in mind.

ADVANTAGES	DISADVANTAGES
Recovery of VAT on VAT returns (see Chapter 5).	Possible depression of profitability if customers can't recover VAT.
Might make your business look bigger than it is and give additional credibility as a result.	Additional bookkeeping and administration in compliance with VAT regulations.
There may be some cash flow planning available in relation to VAT payments.	Possible negative cash flow issues.
Possible gains through the operation of the flat rate scheme (see Chapter 3).	Penalties are imposed for mistake and errors in VAT compliance.

The main advantage of being registered for most businesses will be the right to reclaim VAT paid on costs. This is also know as "input tax", and, as you would expect, there are plenty of rules and restrictions on claiming it (see Chapter 5).

The main disadvantage to registration is the possible loss of trade because of having to add VAT to your prices to customers who can't reclaim VAT. Where you keep your prices the same after registration, you risk reduced profitability.

EXAMPLE

Ellie Enfield runs a hairdressing salon. Her turnover is £72,000 and so she does not have to be VAT registered. The costs of running the business are £44,000 including VAT of £3,300. Her annual profit is £28,000.

Ellie takes on a part-time manicurist and her turnover increases to £78,000 and so she must register for VAT. Unfortunately for Ellie, she can't suddenly put up all her prices by 20% to account for the VAT, as her customers won't tolerate such an increase. A lady who is happy to pay £40 to have her hair cut is unlikely to accept an overnight price rise to £48. As a result, Ellie decides to keep her prices at existing rates, at least for now, which means she has to foot the bill for the VAT due.

This means that her gross turnover of £78,000 now becomes £65,000 plus VAT at 20% (£13,000). Her costs have increased slightly to £46,500, including VAT of £3,500 which she is able to reclaim thereby reducing them to £43,000 net. The overall effect is that her turnover has increased by £6,000 but her profit for the year has decreased by £6,000!

	Before registration (£)	After registration (£)
Gross turnover	72,000.00	78,000.00
VAT	Nil	13,000.00
Net turnover	72,000.00	65,000.00
Gross expenditure	44,000.00	46,500.00
VAT	3,300.00	3,500.00
Net expenditure	44,000.00	43,000.00
Profit	28,000.00	22,000.00

Had she done all her work for a VAT-registered business, say, as a freelance hairdresser to a film company registering and charging VAT, it's unlikely to result in the same problem. This is because the film company can recover VAT and so they wouldn't worry about VAT being added to their bills. As a registered person she would have the advantage of being able to recover the VAT on her costs, i.e. £3,500, and there's no cost to her in respect of the VAT she charges. In fact, she gets to keep the VAT she charges her customers in her bank account for up to three months at which time she has to pay it over to the VATman. So rather than her profit dropping, it actually leaps to £35,000.

	(£)
Gross turnover	93,600
VAT	15,600
Net turnover	78,000
Gross expenditure	46,500
VAT	3,500
Net expenditure	43,000
Profit	35,000

1.1.6.   Can registration be avoided?

If registration is not going to be good for your business, is there anything you can do to avoid it?

One important point is that the VAT registration rules only apply to businesses. This means that if your activity is really just a hobby then they do not apply. One of the earliest tribunal cases looked at just this point. Lord Fisher had an estate in Norfolk and ran a pheasant shoot each year. It cost a lot of money to breed the birds, employ the staff and arrange the shooting so he asked his "guests" to give him something to contribute to the costs incurred. The VATman decided that this was a business and Lord Fisher appealed saying that he was just a chap having a bit of fun with his chums and asking them for a contribution. The tribunal agreed with him and set out the factors that they think should be taken into account in deciding whether or not a business exists for VAT purposes.

These are:

1. Is it a serious undertaking, earnestly pursued - how is the activity organised and run?

2. Is there reasonable or recognisable continuity - is this activity ongoing rather than just occasional?

3. Does it have substance - how many transactions are there and how big are they?

4. Is consideration received and given - is the activity primarily involved with making supplies for payment?

5. Is it commercial - are the supplies of the sort that are made by other commercial providers and is the activity run along similar lines?

6. Is there a profit motive - is the making of a profit an aim?

EXAMPLE

Graham Grimsby is a keen collector of vintage toys. Occasionally he sells a toy either to raise funds to purchase something else he really wants or simply to make room. His activity has no real substance, is not done to make a profit and is certainly not run on business lines. This is a hobby and so the VAT rules are of no concern. However, if he realised that he was making money on his occasional sales, he might be tempted to start buying with resale in mind. If he keeps doing this, at some point he will stop being an individual with a hobby and become a businessman dealing in toys. At that point, VAT becomes a real issue for him to consider.

TIP

If you wish to avoid registration by arguing that your activity is not a business but a hobby, you're more likely to succeed if you concentrate your argument around the six factors mentioned above.

1.1.7. Can a business be reorganised to escape registration?

Of course, the simplest answer for many businesses is to keep your turnover below the registration limit. We have seen that the impact on Ellie would be so significant that she would be much worse off by taking on her manicurist and increasing turnover by £5,000. Staying small is actually better for her, but if this is not an option what can she do?

An alternative might be to split her business into more than one entity. Let's think again about Donald Derby. His problem was that he had two trades being operated by the same person (himself). Could he perhaps run his consultancy business through a limited company and leave his garden opening in his own name as a sole trader? Would this keep both businesses below the registration limit and so avoid the need to worry about VAT registration? The answer is "yes". Remember that registration is by reference to the total turnover of all businesses run by the same person. Companies, partnerships and soles traders are separate persons for VAT purposes and can each have a separate registration limit (currently the full £77,000).

1.1.8. Are there any drawbacks to having more than one VAT registration?

Running businesses through different entities, i.e. partnerships, companies and as a sole trader, sounds like the clear way to avoid VAT registration, but there are a couple of things to bear in mind. Firstly, the costs of running several small businesses are likely to be more than running one larger one. And importantly, the VATman doesn't like it as he'll lose out, so the law gives him powers to say that where a business has artificially been split into smaller ones, he can insist that they be registered as one. However, he's required to prove that the split is artificial, and to do this he has to consider the financial, economic and organisational links between the businesses.

Trap. Businesses artificially split to avoid VAT registration are likely to be attacked, and can mean having to pay arrears of VAT with interest and penalties.

1.1.9. What will the VATman look for where businesses have been split?

Where you run two or more businesses each with turnover below the registration limit, any transactions between them must be made at market value. Make sure that each business acts like a genuine stand-alone enterprise:

- **Discounts.** It can't get discounts from its associates just for being related, but you're allowed to give the same discounts as you would offer to a normal customer.

- **Costs.** Does each business bear its own costs or are they being paid for by a connected company?

> #### TIP
>
> It's OK for one business to buy goods on behalf of other related businesses, say, to benefit from extra discounts for bulk purchases, but it must recharge the cost of these to the other businesses, and at a price no less than the other business could have bought the goods for had it purchased them direct from the supplier.

- **Income.** If income from one business is received by another, this should be in the accounts of the business which books it. So where one business takes the money for a sale made by a related business, perhaps because it's the only one which has the ability to take money by credit card, make sure the money is passed over to the business that actually made the sale, although a small handling charge could be made.

- **Bank accounts.** Each business must have its own account. One company can act as banker for another, but it should make a charge to the other business for providing this service.

- **Accounting records.** Each of the businesses must have their own records.

- **Feasibility.** If looked at in isolation is each business credible? Do they each have the look of commercial enterprises? Do they seek to make a profit?

- **Type of business.** Do the businesses have the same trade but for different customers, e.g. one company supplying VAT-registered customers and another for private clients? There is a clear VAT planning angle here but no commercial justification and so the VATman wouldn't be happy with a business split for this reason alone.

- **Premises and equipment.** Do the businesses share these or have their own? There is nothing wrong or unusual in related companies sharing premises, staff and equipment. However, where they do, it must be clear that the costs are properly shared.

- **Splitting supplies.** Are supplies which would normally be made together being split, e.g. a plumber setting up a company to supply the parts and providing the labour as a sole trader? This is not normal practice so you need to have an explanation as to why it's happening here. The customer's perception can also be important. Does the customer genuinely know and believe that there are two independent suppliers?

- **Trap.** Remember, the VATman has no qualms about telephoning some of your customers and asking them what they think!

- **Timing can be important.** If you start up as two separate entities, then all well and good. But where you wait until turnover is approaching the registration limit and then split the business into two or more parts, it looks suspicious.

1.1.10. Can you register even where turnover is less than the registration limit?

Where your business is wholly or mainly with VAT-registered customers, you'll generally be better off registered for VAT. This is because you would be able to get back the VAT you pay on your costs. As long as this saving outweighs the additional costs of being registered, e.g. a bit more bookkeeping, registration can save you money.

The VATman allows any business that makes at least some taxable supplies to register whenever it wants. This is called "voluntary registration". To be allowed to register, all you have to do is make some taxable supplies.

1.1.11. Can you choose the date from when you want a voluntary registration to apply?

When registering voluntarily you are able to choose the date from which you wish the registration to be effective. This means that you can pick a date that will maximise reclaiming VAT input tax recovery and minimise output tax liability.

EXAMPLE

If John spends £40,000 plus VAT of £8,000 on supplies for his business in January 2013 but only realises in May 2013 that he could have reclaimed the £8,000 VAT back had he been registered, he can backdate a voluntary registration to January 2013 (he could go back up to four years). But he would have to pay VAT on any supplies (sales) he had made after January. He could go back to his customers and ask for VAT, and, although annoying for them, there would be no net cost to his VAT-registered customers as they can reclaim the retrospective VAT. But unregistered or partially exempt customers wouldn't be able to reclaim the VAT and so John would probably have to meet the cost of this himself.

Trap. A word of warning here. You must choose your date of registration carefully as the VATman won't allow you to change your mind later. The key is to work out how much VAT you will be better off by, through registering on a certain date. This can be done by simply adding up how much you could reclaim on purchases and how much you would have to pay over from sales you've already made.

1.1.12. What's "intending trader" registration?

In some cases you can register even before you've made any taxable supplies, as long as you can satisfy the VATman that you intend to make them in future. Typically, intending trader registrations are for businesses that take months or even years to set up and make taxable supplies. This means that VAT you incur on costs can be recovered even where you aren't selling or supplying anything.

TIP

An intending trader registration means you can reclaim VAT on costs as you go along rather than waiting until you make your first sale. So there's a cash flow advantage.

1

Peter Polperrow is a house builder. He establishes a new company to acquire a plot of land in Cornwall. His intention is to seek planning permission to construct new houses on the land and then to sell those houses to the public. It's likely that the process from starting to negotiate the land purchase through the planning application, the build itself and then the marketing phase will take at least a year. Peter could wait until the houses are sold and then register under the normal rules. However, if he did he would lose out, as he would have to fund the VAT on his expenditure for up to a year before being able to recover it. This cash flow disadvantage could be significant. And there's another trap.

Not all input VAT paid on purchases before registration can be reclaimed, e.g. VAT on materials used for the construction. Therefore, Peter could find that much of the VAT incurred in the first few months would not be eligible. But if he registered as an intending trader at the start of the project, he could reclaim VAT throughout the project and ease his cash flow.

1.2. VAT GROUPS

1.2.1. What's a VAT group?

Most businesses will register on their own. Remember that registration is by person and so it is usual for each entity, sole trader, partnership, company etc. to be considered individually. However, UK VAT law allows certain entities to share a registration. The conditions for group registration are:

- the members of a VAT group must all be UK corporate bodies. This means companies limited by share or guarantee and limited liability partnerships

- the group members must all be established in the UK

- someone must have control over all of the members. This could be one of the members controlling each of the others or an external person (another company individual or partnership) controlling them all. Control means having more than 50% of the voting powers for a company.

1.2.2. Is group registration compulsory?

Group registration is voluntary and quite flexible. If companies do not wish to form a group, they are not required to do so simply because they are eligible. Companies controlled by the same person or another company can be excluded from a group registration.

1.2.3. Which group company is responsible for completing the VAT returns?

When applying for group registration, one of the companies must be designated as the representative member of the group.

The consequences of grouping are:

- there's only one VAT number for all of the members (any pre-existing registrations are cancelled)
- there's only one VAT return to cover all of the supplies made by any group member
- all supplies made to or by group members are treated as supplied to or by the representative member
- all supplies between the group members are ignored for VAT purposes
- group members become jointly and severally liable for any VAT debts of group members.

There are advantages and disadvantages to VAT grouping:

ADVANTAGES	DISADVANTAGES
One VAT number - there's no need to be concerned about getting the right number on invoices and other documents for different companies.	One VAT number - if companies join the group, their old numbers are cancelled. If those companies had quoted their VAT numbers to suppliers, there will be an administrative cost of producing new paperwork, invoices, etc.
One VAT return - there's only one return submission deadline and all the group companies' figures are reflected upon it.	One VAT return - administratively it can be challenging to consolidate and co-ordinate the data from several systems in time for submission.
Intra-group supplies are ignored and so cash flow can be improved and real savings made for exempt and partly-exempt businesses.	Intra-group supplies ignored - it can be confusing having some supplies subject to VAT and others not, even though they are the same goods or services.
Error adjustments - the higher the turnover on VAT returns, the greater the size of error which can be adjusted without the need for separate disclosure to HMRC. And by including more companies, overall turnover increases.	Joint and several liability - problems arising in one company will infect all the others. If the companies were separately registered, this wouldn't happen.

EXAMPLE

Immie Immingham has four companies.

1. Immie Exports exports bicycles and parts to non-EU customers. All of its income is zero-rated and it submits monthly VAT returns.

2. Immie Trading sells the same product range within the UK and charges VAT. It submits quarterly VAT returns.

3. Immie Management is a service company bearing general costs for the other companies and recharging them quarterly. It too is registered for VAT and submits quarterly returns.

4. Immie Finance is a financing company which lent Immie Trading its initial start-up capital. It receives only exempt interest and so is not registered.

If Immie leaves her companies to look after their own VAT, Trading and Management will make payments of VAT to HMRC each quarter. Exports will make a claim each month and Finance will bear VAT as a cost on its purchases as it goes along.

Trap. Part of the VAT cost that Finance has to meet and can't reclaim relates to the charge that Management makes to it. In other words, the VAT costs are self-generated and can't be reclaimed.

If Immie formed a VAT group consisting of Management and Finance, the VAT loss created by the recharge would be eliminated as supplies made between group companies are ignored for VAT purposes. The group would be partly VAT exempt and its claims for input VAT would be restricted, but this loss would be less than they were before the VAT group was formed. But Immie could even improve on this.

If Immie added Trading to the group, there would be a further VAT saving. The group would no longer be partly exempt as the only exempt income (the interest on the loan from Finance to Trading) would now be generated within the group and also ignored. Full input tax recovery would be achieved.

There would then be two registrations and two sets of returns. The group would pay quarterly and Exports would continue to recover monthly. If this was the best solution in cash flow terms she could continue in this structure. If she felt that cash flow would be better with Exports in the group, she could bring it in at any time.

1.2.4.   What are the key factors in deciding on a VAT group structure?

When deciding whether to bring a company into a VAT group, cash flow and absolute savings should be worked out carefully.

Tip

The timing of the introduction of a company into a group is important. For example, where a company wants to eliminate the VAT on a management charge, it should be included in the group before the charge is made.

Trap. Further, because all VAT registrations of companies joining the group are cancelled at the date of entry, this will mean a final VAT return for the company under the old registration number will be needed. If this was for a shorter than usual period, it can result in VAT becoming due earlier than usual. So consider when to add a company to a VAT group carefully so as not to trigger a VAT payment earlier than need be.

1.2.5.   What's "divisional registration"?

Divisional registration is an administrative concession for companies which find it difficult to complete their VAT returns because they operate in several different geographical locations and with differing accounting systems. It's rather like the opposite of group registration in that it allows a single entity, i.e. company, partnership or sole trader, which has a number of different branches (divisions) to send in separate VAT returns using a different VAT registration for each branch, even though strictly it should submit one VAT return to cover all of them.

This facility is only available for fully taxable companies and not partly-exempt ones, and all divisions have to be individually registered even if they wouldn't be required to be registered if looked at on their own.

1.3.   HOW TO REGISTER

1.3.1.   How do you make an application for VAT registration?

You are now required to submit an application for registration online.

For the majority of applications use Form VAT1. In addition to this, Form VAT2 is necessary for partnerships. These forms can be downloaded from HMRC's website http://search2.hmrc.gov.uk/kbroker/hmrc/forms/vatforms.jsp

Applications for VAT group registration also require Form VAT1, VAT50 (to establish the group) and VAT51 (one for each group member).

Once submitted, HRMC will process the application and either allow the registration based on the form data or ask for more information.

Trap. If they do seek further information, it's vital that a response is sent within the time limit given. If this is not done, HMRC will usually treat the application as if it has been withdrawn and not proceed with the registration. When you finally get around to answering the query, they will insist on a fresh application being made which could mean that you are treated as late in notifying your liability and become liable to a penalty.

1.3.2. What are "VAT return dates"?

Once a business is VAT registered it will start to receive VAT returns periodically. For most businesses these will cover three-month periods decided by the VATman. Similar businesses generally have the same VAT periods. So, all pubs tend to have the same VAT return period, as will car dealers, banks and so on. The reason for this is that it makes it easier for the VATman to compare the VAT return profiles of different businesses with the same activity. If your VAT returns look different, e.g. you claim back more input tax than average, that could be a basis for a visit.

The VAT return schedules are arranged in so-called staggers:

STAGGER	PERIODS ENDING
Stagger one	March, June, September, December
Stagger two	April, July, October, January
Stagger three	May, August, November, February

1.3.3. Can you change the VAT period?

If you wish to change your VAT return dates, you can ask HMRC to arrange this.

TIP

There can be a financial advantage to changing your VAT period.

EXAMPLE

Adrian Aberdeen has two commercial properties that he rents out. He charges VAT on the rents. The rents are due on the standard quarter days, March 25, June 24, September 29 and December 25. If his VAT returns are in line with Stagger one (see the table above), all of the VAT he collects at each rent day will be payable to HMRC on the same VAT return. The rent collected on March 25 will be payable to HMRC on the March return. For example, if he asked HMRC to move his business onto Stagger three, he would collect the rents and then have use of the VAT until he submitted the May return. That's two full months later!

TIP

You can tell the VATman which stagger you wish to have at the time you make your registration just by indicating this on your application Form VAT1. If you want to change it later, you can just write to him or use Form VAT484, which you can download from his website http://search2.hmrc.gov.uk/kbroker/hmrc/forms/vatforms.jsp

1.3.4. Can you choose the length of your VAT returns period?

Many businesses find it easier and more convenient to account to the end of a week rather than a fixed date. As a result, if the end of a month falls on a Tuesday their records do not coincide with the year-end. They perhaps account on a four, five, four-week pattern to approximate to month-ends. If your business is one of these, you can ask for your VAT return periods to end in line with your accounting dates rather than month-ends. This means that you don't have to spend time adjusting figures to reconcile with the VATman's timetable. You need to ask permission to start with and you must inform the VATman of your accounting dates each year in advance so that he can issue returns to coincide.

Businesses which have more input tax than output tax, such as those dealing in zero-rated products or with high levels of exports and supplies to other EU businesses, will find that they are claiming refunds from HMRC each period.

TIP

In order to get your VAT back sooner you can request monthly returns. But it will, of course, increase administration; after all, you'll be filling in three times as many forms.

KEY POINTS

- the VAT registration limit is £77,000 until April 1 2013 at least
- VAT registration applies to a person rather than a business
- there are advantages and disadvantages to registering
- group VAT registration is voluntary and quite flexible. Again, there are advantages and disadvantages to adopting this structure
- when deciding if grouping will be beneficial you need to work out cash flow and absolute savings carefully
- VAT registration needs to be completed online using Form VAT 1
- once registered the business will receive returns periodically, usually every three months - these periods are known as staggers
- you can ask HMRC to change your return dates.

CHAPTER 2

VAT liability

2.1. INTRODUCTION

Where you make a taxable supply of goods or services, there can be a VAT liability, at zero rate, standard rate (20% from January 4 2011) or reduced rate (currently 5%).

Working out whether or not there's a liability on a supply is the starting point for almost everything to do with VAT and so it's of vital importance; charging VAT where you shouldn't can lead to problems for both you and your customers.

Trap. If you don't charge VAT where you should it can be costly, as the VATman will treat your income as if it included the VAT. This could even wipe out all your profit.

2.2. WHAT ARE THE BASIC VAT RULES?

The basic position is simple: all supplies your business makes are subject to VAT at the standard rate of 20% (from January 4 2011) unless there's a specific rule which says you can apply a different rate. These exceptions are included in lists, called schedules, set out in the **VAT Act 1994**. These will often be referred to in the VATman's guidance.

2.3. VAT SPECIAL RATES

In order to decide whether to charge VAT or not you need to familiarise yourself with the lists in the VAT Act 1994.

- Schedule 7A supplies - these will be subject to the reduced rate of VAT, currently 5%
- Schedule 8 supplies - subject to VAT at the zero rate
- Schedule 9 supplies - exempt.

The standard rate, reduced rate and the zero rate are the "taxable" supplies. In other words, they are the ones upon which VAT is charged. This may seem to be a strange statement when looking at the zero rate but strictly you are charging VAT, albeit calculated at 0%, meaning that there is never a positive VAT amount. At first this looks as if it has the same result as the exemption covered in Schedule 9. But there's an important difference which becomes clear when considering the recovery of VAT as input tax (see Chapter 5).

> **TIP**
>
> You're allowed to reclaim the VAT you pay on purchases you use to make taxable supplies, even zero-rated ones, but you can't where the supply is exempt. There are also special rules for reclaiming VAT on purchases which were used to make both taxable and exempt supplies.

2.4. DECIDING WHICH VAT RATE APPLIES

Each schedule is split into "groups", which relate to different types of supply. These give good guidance as to where to look for possible relief. For example, if you need the VAT rate for a new type of biscuit you have created, looking in Schedule 8, Group 1: "Food" is a good bet. Looking in Schedule 9, Group 2: "Insurance" is not going to be much use.

This approach means that you won't waste time looking in places that are irrelevant. The key point to remember is that the headings are just that and do not give all the detail you need; you have to read the whole text carefully before coming to a conclusion. Some of the groups are extremely simple: take Schedule 8, Group 11: "Bank Notes". It consists of one sentence and it's pretty clear what the zero rating applies to.

2.5. USING THE VATMAN'S WEBSITE

It's easy to get liability questions wrong by not reading the whole of the provision carefully. You can find some further help from HMRC who have produced a series of booklets with detailed explanation of the VAT rates, and these are available on the website. Whilst useful, a little bit of scepticism is prudent as the interpretation is theirs and you are perfectly at liberty to interpret the law differently.

Trap. Some of the VATman's publications aren't his interpretation of the law but actually part of the legislation, so in these cases you must accept his view. Where his publications (notices) carry the "force of law", they are clearly marked.

2.6. WHAT ARE THE CONSEQUENCES OF GETTING IT WRONG?

Over the years there have been many cases concerning VAT liability highlighting the consequences of getting it wrong.

2.6.1. Charging business customers VAT unnecessarily

At first sight it might seem sensible to charge VAT just in case. If your customers are VAT registered themselves and can recover the VAT you charge them, then there's no downside. You charge it and pay it to HMRC. Your customer reclaims it and the whole thing is neutral. But, there's a problem here; one of the criteria for reclaiming VAT on VAT returns is that the tax has been correctly charged in the first place.

If you try to reclaim VAT that has been charged in error, the VATman has every right to refuse to pay you. If this happens, the only recourse is to go back to the supplier and ask for a refund. If you are the supplier, you could end up with a lot of extra administration in raising credit notes and repaying customers' VAT.

2.6.2.   Charging private customers VAT unnecessarily

The public, and many businesses, are not registered for VAT and so can't reclaim VAT they pay. Those businesses with exempt income may also suffer a restriction in VAT recovery (see Chapter 5). Adding VAT to supplies for these customers increases the cost and could make you uncompetitive. If you have a rival applying the correct rate, they could be cheaper as a result. If you reduce your price to compete but still account for VAT, your profit is going to be reduced or even eliminated altogether.

2.6.3.   Not charging VAT where you should

Your customers will not be concerned about this; it's the supplier's responsibility to get it right. But the VATman will be very interested if he spots it. He will treat your income as VAT inclusive and issue an assessment demanding you pay the VAT element to him. Interest and possibly penalties will also be due. The cost of this assessment will fall on you unless you can go back to your customers and ask for the VAT amount on top of what they've already paid. Assuming that you can identify your customers, you will struggle if you are a retailer, you could seek to collect an amount equal to the VAT from them. Your business customers, who can recover VAT charged to them, might be prepared to co-operate, but those who can't claim it back will be less willing, and you're unlikely to be able to force them to do so unless your contract allows for it.

> **TIP**
>
> The price you show in a contract is deemed to include VAT unless it specifies otherwise. So, include a clause which says that where VAT is subsequently found to be due you can charge this to the customer.

2.7.   NO VAT TRAP

One trap that businesses fall into is to assume that if they pay VAT on something when they buy it, they should charge VAT when they sell it or recharge it in some other way. The converse is even more common, i.e. not charging VAT to a customer because you didn't pay VAT on purchase; this is equally wrong.

Helen Harrogate runs a shop selling ladies and girls clothing. She bought some dresses from the manufacturer. The dresses came with matching handbags. The manufacturer believed that the zero rating for the dresses would cover the bags as well and so charged no VAT. Helen assumed that the manufacturer was correct and zero-rated the sales in the shop. HMRC visited the manufacturer and assessed for VAT on the bags. The manufacturer raised an invoice to Helen to pass on the VAT cost and Helen wasn't concerned as she could reclaim it on her next VAT return. The VATman then came to see Helen (and all the manufacturer's other customers) and assessed her for the VAT she had not charged and declared on her sales. She had no way of passing this cost on to her customers and so had to pay the tax herself.

TIP

Know your trade and do your homework - the above scenario is a classic example of why you should be sure you understand the VAT treatment of the products you sell.

2.8. THE CHANGING NATURE OF GOODS

Some items will pass through a business and change character in the process. A restaurant will buy in zero-rated food products but turn them into meals which are standard-rated. A printer will buy standard-rated paper and ink but sell zero-rated books.

TIP

Always consider what you are supplying rather than what is supplied to you.

2.9. SUPPLIES OUTSIDE THE SCOPE OF VAT

A supply can be outside the scope of VAT altogether, e.g. goods traded outside the EU area. If this is the case, then the concept of a supply being taxable or exempt and having to decide what rate is applicable is irrelevant. VAT law sets out the scope of VAT as follows:

"VAT shall be charged on any supply of goods or services made in the United Kingdom, where it is a taxable supply made by a taxable person in the course or furtherance of any business carried on by him." (S.4 of the VAT Act 1994.)

This part of the legislation creates five key factors that must be met before VAT can be due:

1. There has to be a supply of goods or services.

2. The supply must be made in the UK.

3. The supply must be a taxable supply, i.e. not exempt.

4. The person making it must be a taxable person, i.e. registered or required to be registered.

5. There has to be a business motive.

In summary, supplies are outside the scope of the tax where they're made by a person who isn't registered or required to be registered for VAT, they take place outside the UK, or they are not made in the course of business, e.g. they are being made as part of a hobby.

2.9.1. What are the effects of making outside-the-scope supplies?

If income is outside the scope of VAT because there's no supply involved, no business motive or it would all be exempt from VAT, the value does not count towards the registration limit, nor can registration be made on a voluntary basis if this is the only source of income.

If income is outside the scope of VAT for any other reason, it does not count towards the compulsory VAT registration limit but registration could be put in place on a voluntary basis in most circumstances.

EXAMPLE

Angus Aberdeen is a fishery consultant. All of his clients are Norwegian. His income is outside the scope of VAT as his supplies are treated as taking place in Norway. Even though his turnover is £150,000, he does not have to register for VAT as his supplies do not count towards the registration limit. He could register voluntarily if he wished because his supplies would be taxable if made in the UK.

TIP

It will be to your financial advantage to register voluntarily where you incur VAT on UK expenditure which bears VAT, as you'll be able to reclaim this like any trader who is required to register.

VAT liability

- there are currently three VAT rates: standard (20% from January 4 2011), reduced (5%) most commonly applying to utility costs, e.g. electricity and gas, and zero
- the standard rate applies unless the legislation specifies a different one
- charging VAT when you shouldn't can get you into as much trouble with the VATman as not charging it when you should
- some supplies of goods and services are exempt; these are set out in the VAT Act 1994 schedules
- some supplies are outside the scope of VAT, mainly where they are made outside the EU
- you can register for VAT even where the value of VATable supplies you make is below the registration limit.

CHAPTER 3

Special accounting schemes

3.1. INTRODUCTION

Most businesses account for VAT based on when they issue their invoices for sales and receive those for purchases. While this seems simple, it can create trouble. Accounting for output tax because you have raised an invoice is all well and good but it can mean that you pay the VATman before you've been paid by your customer. And sometimes for the purchases you make there might not even be an invoice, e.g. in the case of public payphones or Internet access. But the good news is that there's a host of schemes designed to help businesses that find the normal method of accounting difficult, impossible or just too costly.

3.2. THE FLAT RATE SCHEME (FRS)

3.2.1. Using the FRS

The FRS is a simplified way of calculating the VAT you have to declare and pay. And it can actually reduce your VAT bill. It works by charging VAT at the full normal rate on sales you make but paying over a lower percentage to the VATman. The lower percentage is set by the VATman and varies from time to time. But using the FRS isn't all in your favour, it also means that, with a few exceptions, you can't reclaim any VAT which you pay on purchases.

The FRS makes bookkeeping for VAT simpler, so there can be administrative as well as cost savings.

EXAMPLE

Owen Oswestry is a freelance journalist. He writes for a variety of magazines and newspapers working mainly from home and doing most of his research online. His turnover is £120,000 per annum on which he charges VAT at 20%. His costs are relatively low, being his broadband and telephone lines, IT costs and a little travel. Overall, he incurs VAT on £15,000 of costs. Under normal VAT accounting he would have output tax of £24,000 (£120,000 x 20%) less input tax of £3,000 (£15,000 x 20%) giving an overall liability of £21,000. The flat rate percentage for journalists is 12.5% and so under the flat rate scheme he would pay £18,000, a saving of £3,000 every year.

3.2.2. Who can join the scheme?

The scheme is designed for small businesses, and so you can only join if you anticipate that in the following twelve months your "taxable" turnover (standard, reduced and zero-rated income) will be no more than £150,000.

Trap. The turnover limit is VAT inclusive, i.e. £150,000 including VAT.

3.2.3. Exclusions from the FRS

Some businesses are prohibited from joining the scheme, and it would make some others much worse off meaning that it would be imprudent to join it.

Businesses excluded are those:

- required to use the VAT Tour Operators Margin Scheme (TOMS) (see Chapter 14)
- using any other VAT margin scheme
- subject to the capital goods scheme (see Chapter 7)
- who have left the scheme within the last twelve months
- that have committed offences in relation to VAT
- certain companies eligible for VAT grouping
- repayment businesses, i.e. those whose input tax regularly exceeds their output tax.

3.2.4. Should you join the FRS?

There are two factors in deciding whether it's a good idea to join the FRS: the extent of the administrative saving and the effect on the overall VAT payable to HMRC.

The first thing to do is assess whether it will be easier to complete VAT returns under the scheme. Most businesses will find that it is. Secondly, you need to calculate the amount that is likely to be due to HMRC under the scheme and compare it to that which would be due under normal accounting.

TIP

Don't just weigh up the time saving and direct reduction of VAT costs when considering the FRS. You should also look at the potential for saving the administrative costs of preparing VAT returns.

EXAMPLE

Lewis Llangollen runs a pub. His bookkeeper prepares his VAT returns for him. She charges him £200 per quarter for this. She agrees that if he joins the scheme, her job will be simpler and reduces her fee to £120 per quarter. Under the scheme Llewellyn will be £320 better off each year as a result. Even if he would pay the same VAT amount under the scheme, he may as well join.

3.2.5.   Working out the VAT payable under the FRS

The scheme operates by applying a fixed percentage of VAT to gross turnover. This is the rate you'll have to pay to the VATman on all the supplies you make. The VATman has published a table of rates applying to different types of business. These range from 4% to 14.5%. You need to find the one which applies to the type of business you conduct.

TIP

A 1% reduction in the usual FRS rate applicable to all businesses applies for businesses using the scheme in the first year of VAT registration. Don't confuse this with the first year in which you use the FRS. For instance, an advertising agency adopting the scheme from the date of VAT registration will pay 10% rather than 11% for a full year. But if it had started using the scheme six months after VAT registration, the reduction only applies for six months.

For a table detailing the different FRS rates see Appendix 2.

3.2.6.   Composite or complimentary trades

EXAMPLE

Let's think more about Lewis. The flat rate percentage for pubs is 6.5%. If he has VAT-inclusive turnover of £120,000, he will pay £7,800 VAT in the year. Does it matter that he also sells bar meals? The answer is "no", as long as his trade is that of a pub with food and that he doesn't overstep an invisible line to become a restaurant with a bar. The flat rate percentage for restaurants is much higher: 12.5%. If he is classed as a restaurant rather than a pub, his annual VAT liability will be £15,000, £7,200 more. The difference in FRS rates reflects the fact that a restaurant has higher non-VAT bearing costs than a pub, i.e. the zero-rated food, and so would have a higher net liability under normal rules.

TIP

Where you operate a composite trade, e.g. a pub which serves food, the FRS rate you should use is the one that's most applicable to your trade. This can give you an advantage where the rate for your secondary trade is higher. You might want to develop that side of the business to make the most of this. But be careful that you don't shift the balance so that the secondary trade becomes the primary one, as this would require you to use the percentage applicable.

Special accounting schemes

3

3.2.7. More than one business activity

Mixed businesses are required to use the rate applicable to the largest part of the business. They must monitor the relative sizes of the different trades and change rates if necessary. Sudden changes in businesses are to be reacted to immediately; gradual changes are to be addressed annually.

EXAMPLE

Molly Morpeth has a small veterinary practice with a turnover of £90,000. She applies the flat rate percentage for vets, being 11%. She has a plot of land behind the surgery and develops this over a period of time to provide a kennelling facility. She builds this up over a few years, adding more kennels as she can afford to. Whilst the income from kennelling is less than that from the vet practice she continues to apply the 11% rate. However, she finds that she prefers this part of the business and spends more time on it, reducing the hours she does in the surgery. After five years she finds that her income from kennelling has risen to £90,000 whilst her income from the veterinary service has dropped to £80,000. As the turnover from the kennelling aspect of the business is now higher, she must apply the rate appropriate to the boarding of animals: 12%.

Trap. It can pay to run two trades side-by-side. If Molly had closed the veterinary business and re-opened as a boarding kennel, the 12% rate would have applied immediately as the change was sudden and not gradual.

3.2.8. Reclaiming VAT on costs under the FRS

As we've seen, the scheme works through the application of a fixed percentage to gross turnover. Whatever figure is calculated in this way is the amount due to HMRC. The actual amounts of VAT charged to customers and paid to suppliers are irrelevant. The differing flat rate percentages reflect the typical ratio between output tax and input tax in differing types of business, so an accountant who has low input tax pays a high flat rate of 14.5% whereas a petrol station with high input tax pays a low flat rate of 6.5%.

Trap. Where a business incurs significant amounts of expenditure, it might end up worse off. For example, for a business where the FRS rate applicable is 14.5% the most output tax it could save would be £6,875. That's £125,000 (i.e. the maximum turnover permitted under the FRS ignoring VAT) x 5.5% (20% standard rate minus the discounted FRS rate of 14.5%). So if it incurred input tax on its purchases of £8,000, it would be worse off joining the FRS.

Special accounting schemes

3

3.2.9. The capital expenses rule

The general rule that prevents you from reclaiming VAT on purchases is overridden where you make a single purchase of any capital items, e.g. a computer in excess of £2,000 (including VAT). In this situation you can reclaim the VAT on the purchase despite using the FRS.

TIP

Where you're considering the purchase of capital equipment just under the £2,000 (including VAT) mark, it can save you money by choosing a product that costs just over this limit, e.g. the net cost of a computer costing £1,800 (including VAT) would be £1,800 because you can't reclaim the VAT. But the net cost of a computer costing £2,100 would be £1,750 because you can reclaim the VAT of £350. Not only that, you'll probably be getting a better product.

Trap. Where the exception applies to an asset and the VAT was reclaimed, if you sell the asset, you'll have to charge and account to the VATman for output tax at the full rate.

3.2.10. Application of FRS rate to gross turnover

The flat rate percentage is applied to gross turnover, i.e. total turnover including any VAT. The implementation of the scheme is all internal and at the accounting and VAT return preparation stage. All dealings with the outside world, customers and suppliers will be normal. Thus, an accountant (with a 14.5% flat rate percentage) preparing a set of accounts for a client for £1,000 will still show VAT of £200 at 20% on the invoice, not £145.

Trap. When assessing whether there would be a saving available through joining the scheme, several businesses have used net turnover by mistake and calculated very high savings indeed. Having joined the scheme they then find that the anticipated savings simply do not exist. As it's not possible to backdate a withdrawal from the scheme, it's vital that from time to time you compare the VAT you would have paid if you didn't operate the FRS with that which you are paying under the scheme, and leave it if it's not saving you money.

Trap. Gross turnover includes income that would not otherwise bear tax. If a business makes zero or reduced-rate supplies, the flat rate percentage for that trade sector must take these into account as part of the FRS turnover. This can create a cost if you make supplies with a significant value that would be exempt from VAT or zero-rated if you weren't using the FRS, e.g. rental income or even the bank interest you receive must be subjected to the FRS rate.

Special accounting schemes

Reg Ripon owns a shop selling bicycles and accessories. Above the shop are four flats that he also owns and rents out. Income from the shop is £130,000, and £16,000 from the flats. Under normal accounting, VAT is due at the standard rate on the income from the shop and the rent is exempt. Under the FRS, the rate of 6.5% applies to total income of £146,000 which means that Reg has to hand over 6.5% VAT to HMRC on the rents he receives even though he hasn't charged a penny to his tenants.

TIP

If you're in the FRS and about to make an exempt or zero-rated transaction with a high value, e.g. the sale of a property, consider leaving the scheme beforehand. This way you'll avoid having to account for VAT at the FRS rate on it.

3.2.11.   Applying to join the FRS

You can only use the FRS after receiving permission from the VATman. Joining the scheme is by application using Form VAT 600 FRS.

Download Zone

For a weblink to **Form VAT 600 FRS**, visit **http://books.indicator.co.uk**. You'll find the access code on page 2 of this book.

3.2.12.   Leaving the FRS

You can voluntarily leave the FRS at any time, but a business must leave the scheme when gross turnover has exceeded £230,000 in the previous twelve months unless you can show the VATman that this was due to unusual circumstances and that turnover in the following twelve months will be below £191,500.

A business must leave the scheme if turnover will exceed £230,000 in the next 30 days alone.

There's no form needed to notify the VATman that you no longer want or can use the FRS, but you should tell him in writing when you do.

3.3.   CASH ACCOUNTING

The cash accounting scheme can provide cash flow benefits. It's relatively simple to operate and gives you a VAT advantage where you have customers that are slow payers and/or become bad debtors.

3.3.1. How does it work?

Rather than output and input tax being accounted for in the VAT return period in which you raise your invoices on sales or receive those on purchases, you account for these only when your customer pays you and when you pay your bills.

3.3.2. Who can use cash accounting?

Businesses with a turnover up to £1,350,000 can join the scheme. There's no application process, eligible businesses can simply start using it. However, there are some businesses which will not be eligible:

- those that are behind with VAT return submission

- those with significant or rising VAT debts

- those which have previously committed VAT offences or have had the use of the scheme withdrawn in the previous twelve months.

3.3.3. Does the scheme cover all supplies?

There are some types of supply which must be accounted for outside of the scheme. The main ones are:

- HP and similar sales

- transactions involving other countries in the EC

- sales with long credit periods (in excess of six months); and

- supplies where invoices are raised before the supply is made.

This doesn't mean that a business with such supplies can't use the cash accounting scheme, merely that the supplies which are excluded must be accounted for outside it. Thus, some businesses can have part of their activity within the scheme and part under normal accounting.

3.3.4. Is cash accounting good for all types of business?

The answer is an emphatic "no". The big advantage of cash accounting is that you only pay VAT over to the VATman when you have been paid by your customers. In this way you never get into a situation where you have to fund the VAT out of your own resources. But you can change the timing of VAT payments even under the normal invoice-based accounting method by creating a "tax point" that defers when VAT is payable (see Chapter 4). Cash accounting could therefore disadvantage you.

Special accounting schemes

At Lewis Llangollen's pub his customers all pay him in cash or by credit card when he serves them. Therefore, he always has payment at the time VAT output tax is triggered. Cash accounting would be of no benefit to him as it wouldn't defer the payment of output tax he has to make to the VATman. Plus, he's entitled to reclaim input tax on his purchases as soon as he receives the purchase invoice. If he used cash accounting, he would have to wait until the VAT return period in which he paid the invoices before he could claim the input tax back. Cash accounting would actually be bad for cash flow.

Trap. Generally, cash accounting isn't worthwhile for retailers or businesses which can exploit the continuous supply tax point rules (see Chapter 4).

3.3.5. What counts as a receipt of payment for cash accounting?

Cash	Date of receipt unless received by someone acting as your agent, in which case it's the date they received payment on your behalf.
Cheque	The date you received the cheque or the date of the cheque (whichever is later), not the date it's cleared.
Bank transfer	The date your account is credited.
Credit/debit card	The date the card is processed or voucher created.
Part payment	The date the part payment is received. If the payment relates to a supply which includes different rates of VAT, an apportionment is to be made.

3.3.6. Claiming input tax

The same payment rules apply to input tax claims. For payments by cheque, credit or debit card or bank transfer, there will be plenty of evidence of payment to justify the input tax claim.

TIP

For cash payments, it's necessary to get the supplier to issue a receipt that clearly acknowledges payment, not just an invoice which shows that a supply has been made.

3.3.7. Leaving the scheme

Once in the scheme, a business' turnover can increase to £1.6 million before it is required to leave. It must also leave if it ceases to trade and cancels its VAT registration. A business can leave voluntarily at an earlier date if it chooses to.

Where it leaves the scheme because it's cancelling its registration, it must apply the normal rules to any invoices and bills outstanding at that date. So, where there have been sales and a tax point thereby created, but payment not received from the customer, the output tax is due to the VATman in the return period the registration is cancelled. Similarly, any VAT on purchase invoices on hand at the time registration is cancelled but not yet paid can be claimed in the same period.

TIP

If your business leaves the scheme but continues to trade, you have a choice: you can account for the VAT in the same way as if you were ceasing to trade or continue to treat pre-cessation supplies under the cash accounting rules for up to six months.

EXAMPLE

Donald Dundee has a company that manufactures telescopes. The company has used cash accounting previously but turnover has exceeded the £1.6m exit level as at March 31. At that date there were debtors of £90,000 including VAT of £15,000. The company could pay this liability immediately if it wished to. Instead, it takes advantage of the six-month rule. In the VAT return period to June 30, £60,000 of these debts is collected and so £10,000 output tax is added to the return VAT liability. In the period to September 30 a further £24,000 is collected. This includes £4,000 VAT and this is added to the return output tax. Whilst there is still an outstanding amount of £6,000, the company must account for the output tax on this as well as it has now reached the six-month limit. A further £1,000 is therefore due on the September return.

3.4. ANNUAL ACCOUNTING

Annual accounting is designed for businesses that want to simplify administration by allowing the submission of only one VAT return each year rather than four.

3.4.1. Who can use annual accounting?

Any business with a turnover of up to £1,350,000 unless it's in a VAT group, has ceased using the scheme in the previous twelve months, has a significant or rising debt or has committed a VAT offence.

If turnover exceeds £100,000 per annum, the business must have been VAT registered for at least twelve months before joining.

3.4.2.   What are the benefits of using annual accounting?

Ease of administration. There is only one VAT return to complete each year instead of four and you get two months to submit it instead of one.

Fixed payments throughout the year. Whilst there is only one return you still make payments as you go along. These are based on the previous year's return liability. Knowing how much you will pay each month allows for secure cash flow planning.

TIP

Growing businesses can delay accounting for VAT by using the annual accounting scheme because they only have to make payments to the VATman based on the previous year's figures, which will of course be less than the amounts actually due. A balancing payment only becomes due when the annual return is completed.

TIP

Possibly the biggest advantage of the scheme is that you can choose your own annual accounting year. This means that if you have a marked seasonal trade you can achieve significant cash flow gains by choosing your VAT return period to start at the very beginning of your seasonal boom.

EXAMPLE

Carly Carlisle grows and sells Christmas trees and has a turnover of £900,000 including VAT of £150,000. Due to the nature of her business, all of her income is received in December. If she had VAT returns covering normal calendar quarters she would pay all of the VAT to the VATman in January. If she adopts annual accounting and chooses December 1 for her accounting year, she will gain significantly.

MONTH	NORMAL ACCOUNTING (£)	ANNUAL ACCOUNTING (£)
January	150,000	
February		
March		37,500
April		
May		
June		37,500
July		
August		
September		37,500

Month	Normal accounting (£)	Annual accounting (£)
October		
November		
December		
January		37,500
Total	**150,000**	**150,000**

This example shows Carly making three payments of £37,500 followed by a further balancing payment two months after the year-end in the January of the following year. She has had use of the VAT for an average of six months longer than would otherwise have been the case.

3.4.3. Are there any disadvantages of annual accounting?

Some businesses find that the discipline of completing a VAT return each quarter means that they have to keep their records up-to-date and accurate. If this requirement is not there, some get a little behind and lose track of where the business is going. If less is paid during the year than would be the case under normal rules, e.g. because turnover has increased over the previous year, an additional balancing payment will be due with the return. This can come as a shock if you are not keeping track of your liability as you go along. And where you do not have sufficient funds to pay the return liability, you could fall foul of the penalty regime.

Trap. If your business is turning over less this year than last, it will still have to make its regular payments based on the previous year. This can mean that more is being paid than is strictly due giving rise to cash flow difficulties.

Trap. If the business makes significant one-off purchases of assets or stock, it will get no immediate credit for this but will have to wait for the annual VAT return. If this is some months away, it could be costly.

3.4.4. Joining the scheme

Application for joining the annual accounting scheme is done by completing Form VAT 600 AA.

Download Zone

For a weblink to **Form VAT 600AA**, visit **http://books.indicator.co.uk**. You'll find the access code on page 2 of this book.

3.4.5. Leaving the scheme

A business will be required to leave the scheme where its turnover increases beyond the exit threshold of £1.6m.

3.5. RETAIL SCHEMES - INTRODUCTION

Retail schemes are special methods of calculating liabilities for VAT returns. As their name suggests, they are only intended for use by retailers. There are different types of retail scheme aimed at different sizes of business.

3.5.1. Who can use the schemes?

There's no definition of the term "retailer" in the VAT legislation but it suggests someone who makes the majority of their supplies to the general public, often for cash, cheque or card payment, e.g. shops. The VATman uses a loose definition which can be paraphrased as any business that can't reasonably be expected to account under the normal rules. For instance, the normal rules require every single supply to be identified and VAT accounted for separately. Where there's a high volume of transactions, the normal rules will be difficult and very time consuming to use.

TIP

Retail schemes aren't confined to shops, if you have a high transaction business, e.g. Internet sales, you may also be able to use a retail scheme.

3.5.2. How do the schemes work?

There are a variety of schemes that have different calculation methods. The retailer can choose which method to use, though with some restrictions for the type of business and its turnover.

3.6. POINT OF SALE (POS) SCHEME

The POS scheme is the simplest method of all and is ideal for businesses that have sophisticated tills or where all of the goods are barcoded or tagged. In this way each sale can be identified as to its correct VAT rate at the point of sale.

It's available to retailers with a turnover of up to £130 million.

It's the only retail scheme available where the business' supplies are either all standard or all reduced-rated.

3.6.1. How does the POS scheme work?

The business simply keeps a running total of all sales made and then treats the resultant amount as being VAT inclusive on a daily basis.

EXAMPLE 1

Tim Tenby runs a sweet shop and so all of his income is subject to the standard rate of VAT. At the end of each day he counts up the money in his till and records the total as his sales for the day. His VAT liability is calculated from this. On August 5 he takes £396.00. His liability for that day is £66.00 (£396/6) less any input tax.

EXAMPLE 2

Helen Harrogate has introduced a new till which works in conjunction with a barcode reader and has all of her clothing labelled accordingly. At the end of each day she has an accurate record of what value of sales she has at the standard rate (ladies clothing and all accessories) and the zero rate (girls clothing). On August 5 she has taken £620 of which £580 is standard-rated and £40 zero-rated. Her liability for the day is £96.66 (£580/6) less any input tax incurred. The zero-rated sales give rise to no VAT due to HMRC.

EXAMPLE 3

Dan Dover runs a sandwich shop so much of his income is zero-rated, being cold takeaway food, but there is a large standard-rated element as well, soft drinks, confectionary, eat-in supplies and some hot takeaway food such as coffee. Dan's products are not barcoded or otherwise tagged as to VAT liability. The only way he could identify supplies of differing rates would be through ensuring that different buttons were pressed on the till to evidence different types of sale. Whilst theoretically possible, this could be prone to human error, particularly at busy periods such as lunchtime. It is unlikely that the POS scheme will be appropriate for him.

3.6.2. Valuing the daily takings

There may be many reasons why the amount of money in a till is not the same as that taken in return for sales that day.

Credit sales. If a retailer lets some customers take away goods without paying at that time, they still need to be recorded as sales for the day. They would have to add in the value of sales of this nature as the goods are supplied and then remember to omit their value when the customer later pays.

Contributions from manufacturers for promotional sales. Under certain manufacturer-led promotion schemes, the manufacturer will make a payment to the retailer for running it. This is income for the retailer and VAT is due but, of course, there will be nothing in the till to show it.

Non-cash sales. The value of any non-cash sales must be included in the day's takings. This will include cheques, credit and debit card sales, any electronic payments and other bank transfers and also the value of certain promotional coupons.

Most of these items result in an increase in takings and so an increase in VAT payable. There are some items that may be recorded as sales but later can be taken out again, reducing the liability:

- counterfeit notes
- invalid card transactions
- foreign currency taken in error
- outdated promotional coupons
- trade sales
- refunds
- items showing up as a result of a faulty till
- unsigned or dishonoured cheques
- training entries
- void transactions.

3.7. APPORTIONMENT SCHEMES

If the POS scheme doesn't work for your business, you should consider apportionment schemes. Used in the right circumstances they can reduce the VAT you have to hand over to the VATman.

3.7.1. Apportionment Scheme 1 (APP1)

APP1 is available for businesses with a turnover of up to £1m. It works by calculating the ratio of purchases at the different VAT liabilities and assumes that the same ratio applies to sales. If the mark-up applied to differing product lines is the same, then this method will be highly accurate. If they vary significantly then the resultant tax calculated will be different to that which would be due under normal rules.

EXAMPLE

Consider again Helen Harrogate from our earlier examples. If she didn't have her new till and barcodes she might not feel that the POS scheme would be possible as her shop assistants might not key in differing items to the till correctly. She could use APP1.

Her purchases and notional sales prices in the VAT quarter are as follows:

Item	Purchase Value	Mark-up Rate	Sales Value
Ladies clothes and accessories - standard-rated	£100,000	50%	£150,000
Girls clothing - zero-rated	£50,000	100%	£100,000

Assuming that she sold all of the stock she bought, she would have a VAT liability of £8,333 (output tax of £25,000 (£150,000/6 less input tax of £16,667 (£100,000/6)) under normal rules. Under APP1 she applies the purchase ratio to sales instead. Two-thirds of purchases are standard-rated (£100,000/£150,000) so two-thirds of income is treated as standard-rated. Total income is £250,000, so £166,667 is deemed to include VAT giving output tax of £27,778 (£166,667/6). Deducting the input tax of £16,667 gives a liability of £11,111 under the scheme, £2,778 more than under the normal rules. APP1 is not attractive in this situation.

If her mark-up rates were the other way around and the higher rate applied to the standard-rate goods, the result would be quite different:

Item	Purchase value	Mark-up rate	Sales value
Ladies clothes and accessories - standard-rated	£100,000	100%	£200,000
Girls clothing - zero-rated	£50,000	50%	£75,000

Under normal rules Helen's liability would be £16,667 (output tax £33,334 (£200,000/6) less input tax £16,667 (£100,000/6). Under APP1 it would be £13,889 (output tax of £30,556 (total income of (£275,000 * 2/3)/6) less input tax of £16,667); in other words £2,778 less than under normal rules. APP1 looks very attractive.

Trap. The VATman expects businesses to choose a method that closely replicates the true liability under normal rules, not the one that gives the lowest liability. Whilst he says that you can choose the one that suits your business best, he reserves the right to refuse use of a scheme if it *"does not give a fair and reasonable result"* or *"for the protection of the revenue"*; for which read: *"you are not paying enough!"*

Note. APP1 requires you to carry out a calculation each VAT return period and then do an overall calculation once a year to even out peaks and troughs in buying patterns.

3.7.2. APP1 and self-manufactured goods

One trouble with APP1 is that it doesn't cater for goods you manufacture, or grow, yourself, as these don't have a straightforward purchase price to build into the purchase price ratio calculation. These supplies can't be included in the scheme meaning that you either have a separate calculation for them or you adopt a different scheme in which they can be included.

@@##$$

3.7.3.   Apportionment Scheme 2 (APP2)

The other apportionment scheme, APP2, goes some way to addressing the problems associated with APP1. It can be used by businesses with turnover up to £130m; it too uses a calculated ratio but it uses the ratio of expected sales values, not purchases.

The benefits of APP2 are that:

- it's more accurate

- it caters for differing mark-up rates; and

- it allows for own produced goods and services to be included.

3.7.4.   Calculating the APP2 ratio

The main downside of APP2 is that the calculations involved are more complex. All purchases are marked up to their expected sales price. This sounds simple and, of course, it is if you have very few sales lines or you have consistent mark-up rates across your range of products. However, imagine a shop with, say, 600 different products each with a different mark-up. Your calculation will need 600 lines!

Further, you will need to amend calculations if anything occurs that will alter your expected sales price. If your ratio assumes that you will make 100% on certain lines but you actually only make 50%, then the ratio is inaccurate.

Adjustments will be required for anything that affects the price such as:

- reductions for sell-by dates

- special offers and promotions

- end of line sales

- reductions to clear old stock

- wastage

- breakages

- pilferage.

Finally, APP2 does not have an annual adjustment but operates through using a twelve-month rolling set of figures throughout the year. This means that any imbalances or adjustments needed for one month are corrected the next.

42

© Tried and Tested Ways to Reduce Your VAT Bill, Indicator

Special accounting schemes

3

3.8. DIRECT CALCULATION SCHEMES

3.8.1. Direct Calculation Scheme 1 (DCS1)

DCS1 is available for businesses with a turnover up to £1 million. It works by calculating expected sales for the minority goods in the business, i.e. the goods of the VAT liability which makes up the lowest percentage of sales.

EXAMPLE

Helen from our earlier examples sells more ladies clothing and accessories by value than girls clothing. She would apply her mark-up rates to girls clothing to calculate the expected sales value of this minority. Whatever total she comes to is deducted from her daily gross takings and the remainder assumed to be standard-rated income. This remainder is treated as VAT inclusive for VAT return purposes.

Had Helen sold more girls clothing she would mark up the standard-rated purchase and simply assume that this was her standard-rated income, treating it as VAT inclusive.

Trap. While DCS1 is a simple concept, it can be cumbersome to use when there are many product lines of differing mark-up. The calculation must usually be done by product line wherever possible. Mark up by class of product lines, e.g. all ladies clothing, is allowed but only where:

- mark-up by line is impossible
- the variation between lines is less than 10%
- mark-up rates are reviewed quarterly; and
- the product class is commercially recognised; in other words you can find comparable items on sale elsewhere.

Trap. The DSC1 calculation assumes that all product purchases in the minority goods are sold in the same VAT return period. Where this doesn't happen, it can be highly distortive.

3.8.2. Direct Calculation Scheme 2 (DCS2)

DCS2 is available for businesses with a turnover up to £130m and works in the same way as DCS1 but also includes an opening and closing stock adjustment. It therefore addresses the stock turn period issue that DCS1 fails to. As a result of this, it's a slightly more complicated calculation to use.

Adjustments. As with APP2, both direct calculation schemes use expected sales figures. If anything changes the expected sales price, then adjustments will be required.

3.9. OTHER RETAIL SCHEMES

3.9.1. Bespoke schemes

If turnover exceeds £130m or any of the other schemes do not work for the business for any reason, the retailer will need to negotiate a bespoke scheme with HMRC. This can be based on the other schemes but will address issues specific to that business.

3.9.2. Can different retail schemes be mixed?

It's possible that a business has different trades within it for which different schemes would be most appropriate. Where this is the case, it's possible to use a POS scheme alongside either a DCS or APP scheme, as long as records can be kept to differentiate between goods sold through the different parts of the business.

Similarly, the business might have retail and trade sales. A retail scheme can be used alongside normal accounting.

3.9.3. Switching retail schemes

If a business becomes ineligible to use a particular scheme, perhaps through increased turnover, it will be expected to start using a new one with effect from the end of the VAT return period in which this occurs.

If the business simply decides that another scheme would be more appropriate for it, perhaps because the proportions of different liability goods it sells changes, it will normally be expected to remain in the old scheme until the end of the year. This can be very expensive and so, when choosing your scheme, you should look at future trends as well as current and historic data.

3.9.4. Special retail schemes

There are special schemes available for florists, pharmacists and catering outlets such as sandwich shops.

3.10. THE SECOND-HAND GOODS SCHEME

The second-hand, or used, goods scheme has been created to cater for goods which have a long life and which are bought and resold more often than some other goods. A beef burger is only ever sold once (hopefully!). VAT is added, the burger is eaten and it's gone. On the other hand, a car is bought and VAT charged.

It may then be sold back to the dealer as a part-exchange item when a new car is purchased. The same car might be bought and sold several time throughout its life. Therefore, it would be unreasonable for VAT to be added every time the car is sold.

The second-hand goods scheme addresses this issue by only applying VAT to the profit made on a car each time it's sold.

3.10.1. What goods can be included in the scheme?

The following items are eligible for sale through the scheme:

- goods where VAT was not charged on their purchase, i.e. goods bought from the public, other non-VAT registered people and those already in the scheme when bought
- goods suitable for further use as they are or following repair or restoration
- collectors' items such as used stamps, coins, zoological, botanical and anatomical specimens, historical or archaeological items
- antiques - anything over 100 years old
- works of art.

3.10.2. Basic principles of the scheme

The business keeps a record of purchase and sales prices in order to calculate the profit margin made on each sale. In order to ensure that the correct prices are attributed to each item, a detailed stock record is required.

PURCHASES	STOCK NUMBER
	Date of purchase
	Purchase invoice number
	Purchase price
	Name of seller
	Unique reference number
	Description
Sales	Date of sale
	Sales invoice number
	Name of buyer
	Selling price
Accounting	Margin made
	VAT due

3.10.3. What about the costs incurred on the used item?

It's important to note that the margin is based on the actual price paid for the item; other costs incurred, such as repair, are treated outside of the calculation in the normal way.

Example

Barry Birmingham is a car dealer. He buys a used BMW from a member of the public for £16,000. It has not been looked after particularly well and so he puts on a new set of wheels and has it re-sprayed, all at a cost of £2,000 plus VAT of £400. He sells the car for £19,600. His margin for VAT purposes is £3,600 giving an output tax liability of £600. The VAT incurred on the wheels and paintwork is deductible as input tax, giving a net amount due of £200.

3.10.4. Invoices

Invoices raised for sales of margin scheme items will not show any VAT, but will contain a narrative element stating that the sale is being accounted for within the scheme.

3.10.5. Global accounting scheme for used goods

Transactions in second-hand goods require detailed records. This can be arduous for businesses with high volumes of low value goods. Global accounting is designed to assist here.

It can be used for any items costing less than £500 (excluding aircraft, caravans, motor vehicles and horses and ponies) and uses the total purchase and sales prices of all such items, rather than calculating a profit margin on every item individually.

This simplifies accounting and also has another incidental benefit. Under normal margin scheme rules, VAT is accounted for on the profit margin. If an item is sold at a loss, there's no corresponding VAT credit. Under global accounting loss-making items can be offset.

KEY POINTS

- the VAT flat rate scheme (FRS) can be used by any business with an annual turnover of taxable supplies less than £150,000, or total supplies of less than £187,500
- the FRS reduces the amount of VAT you have to pay over to HMRC on your sales but means you can't reclaim the VAT paid on purchases unless they are capital items costing more than £2,000 (including VAT)
- the FRS rate must be applied to all income of the business, e.g. interest received, not just trading income
- cash accounting can be used by any business with a turnover up to £1,350,000 per year
- VAT on sales under cash accounting is payable for the period in which your customer pays you. You can only reclaim VAT on purchases in the return period you pay for them
- annual accounting means that you only have to complete a VAT return once a year
- under annual accounting you make interim VAT payments each quarter based on the previous year's figures
- there are various schemes for retailers which allow them to calculate VAT payable based on average sales or purchases of products rather than each item sold
- the second-hand goods scheme can be used by any business which sells items that have been sold before, e.g. second-hand cars
- the VAT on the second-hand goods is calculated on the profit margin only, not the full sale price.

CHAPTER 4

Output tax - charging VAT

4.1. TAX POINTS

4.1.1. What are "tax points"?

The term "tax point" is used to define the time at which a supply triggers a VAT charge. This can be important when deciding which return to declare the VAT for a particular supply. If you can delay the tax point, you can delay payment of VAT. And where there's a change in the VAT rate, tax points become even more important, especially if you're a customer who can't reclaim the VAT, e.g. a member of the public or an unregistered trader.

4.1.2. Types of tax point

There are two types of tax point: "basic" and "actual", and the rules differ slightly depending on whether the supply is of goods or services.

4.1.3. Basic tax points

Goods. The basic tax point for goods is the date they are provided to the customer.

Trap. Where you're not delivering the goods, say, because the customer is collecting them, the basic tax point is the date you make the goods available to them.

Services. For services, the basic tax point is the date that the service is performed.

> ### TIP
>
> The word performed means that the service is complete, so a three-day training course is only performed for VAT purposes at the end of the third day when it has been completed. This means where a supply you're making spans the end of a return period, the VAT will fall into the later return. This can work in your favour where you're the one making a supply, but against you where you're the recipient. But you might be able to override the basic tax point with an actual tax point.

4.1.4. Actual tax points

In the following circumstances, basic tax points can be overridden by actual tax points:

- payment before the basic tax point - where payment for a supply is received before a basic tax point is reached, an actual tax point occurs and VAT is due to the extent of the payment. This means that a deposit received prior to delivery of goods or services usually creates a tax point
- the issue of a VAT invoice before the basic tax point
- the issue of an invoice within 14 days after a supply also forms an actual tax point.

> **TIP**
>
> The 14-day period can be extended up to 30 days with the VATman's agreement. To take advantage of this facility, you'll need to write to him explaining why you want the extension to apply.

4.2. INVOICING

It's common for a business to issue invoices that create tax points, which means it will have to pay the VAT on them despite not having received payment from its customers. It's important, therefore, to use the tax point rules to your advantage and invoicing plays an important part in this.

4.2.1. What information must an invoice show?

A VAT invoice must contain a great deal of information about the transaction including:

- a sequential number based on one or more series which uniquely identifies the document
- the time of the supply
- the date of the issue of the document
- the name, address and registration number of the supplier
- the name and address of the person to whom the goods or services are supplied
- a description sufficient to identify the goods or services supplied
- for each description, the quantity of the goods or the extent of the services, and the rate of VAT and the amount payable, excluding VAT, expressed in any currency

- the gross total amount payable, excluding VAT, expressed in any currency
- the rate of any cash discount offered
- the total amount of VAT chargeable, expressed in sterling
- the unit price
- where a margin scheme is applied under s.50A or s.53 of the **Value Added Tax Act 1994**, a relevant reference or any indication that a margin scheme has been applied
- where a VAT invoice relates in whole or part to a supply where the person supplied is liable to pay the tax, a relevant reference or any indication that the supply is one where the customer is liable to pay the tax.

There are two dates required on an invoice: the date of the supply, i.e. the basic tax point, and the date the invoice is issued.

Where the basic tax point is to be overridden by the invoice (see above for the rules on this) it's the date the invoice is sent out to the customer that's relevant and not the date put on the invoice. In other words, creating a document won't change the tax point, it has to be sent to the customer for it to be effective.

EXAMPLE

Douglas Ltd sells office stationery. It ships orders as soon as they come in and normally sends invoices with the goods. In March 2011 the company had some computer problems and was unable to generate invoices although they were still delivering goods. On April 20 their systems were running again and they raised invoices for the shipments that went without paperwork. These invoices will show tax points in March, even though the invoices were issued in April.

The reason for this requirement is to ensure that supplies are reflected in the correct return. The supplies shown on the invoices dated in April need to be reported on the VAT return covering March. Similarly, Douglas Ltd's customers are entitled to recover input tax by reference to the tax point rather than the invoice date if different.

TIP

Where you're producing invoices in the final few days of a VAT return period, you can delay sending them out until the next period. This will mean that the tax point is pushed back into the later VAT quarter and you'll get another three months before you have to pay the VAT over. You should also clearly record the date of issue, otherwise if the VATman checked your records he would assume the date of the invoice was the date of issue.

4.2.2. Timing supplies for a VAT advantage

Where your business makes supplies towards the end of a VAT quarter, you could delay the issue of the corresponding invoices until the next period by overriding the basic tax point with the issue of an invoice within 14 days (or up to 30 days if approved by the VATman); the payment of the VAT to the VATman is also delayed.

EXAMPLE

George of Glasgow Ltd raises invoices for design consultancy monthly in arrears. One of its VAT return periods ends on January 31. If it bills for January on the 31st of the month, the invoice creates a tax point in January. The output tax is declared on the January return and it has to pay the liability even though it has not been paid by its clients. If it waits until February 1, the VAT for the January supplies won't be payable until May 31, three months later, by which time its clients have paid him.

Trap. Delaying the invoice might mean that there's a delay in getting paid by your customer.

4.2.3. "Continuous supply" of services - tax points

Some businesses make continuous supplies to their customers, e.g. accountants, which means working out when a tax point is can be tricky; no basic tax point is created because there's no point at which you can say that a service has been completed. A VAT rule specifically addresses this. It states that, in this case, VAT becomes due at the earlier of receipt of payment or issue of invoice.

TIP

Where you make continuous supplies, it's possible to use a special invoicing system that will defer the VAT tax point for supplies you make until you're paid.

EXAMPLE

George of Glasgow Ltd has open-ended contracts with its clients to provide IT services on an ongoing and ad hoc basis. As the supply is one of continuous services, there's no basic tax point. Issuing an invoice creates a tax point but as a significant number of its clients are slow payers, this causes cash flow problems, not least because the company has to pay the VAT over before it has received its fees. But if it issues a document that's not a VAT invoice, but just a request for payment showing details the value of the

This is not to be confused with cash accounting. Under this scheme, output tax and input tax are only reflected on VAT returns by reference to payment. Here, output tax is delayed until payment has been received but input tax can be claimed based upon the purchase invoice date.

4.2.4. Invoicing in advance

An administrative simplification can be achieved for supplies where you intend to charge your customers for set amounts on a regular basis. For example, this is common in the leasing industry where monthly payments are made in return for the hire of goods. The supplier could issue an invoice each month, but this is burdensome. A single invoice can be raised up to a year in advance, showing the payment dates and the amounts due at each of them. The tax point becomes the payment date and is not overridden by the invoice date.

4.3. DEEMED SUPPLIES

Trap. On some occasions an output tax charge will arise, even though there's no "sale" to a customer.

4.3.1. Transfer of goods

If goods that belong to a business are given away, they are treated as supplied for VAT purposes at that time. This would cover such things as a shop owner taking goods out of the business for his own use, old computer equipment being given away and, of course, gifts.

4.3.2. Business gifts

VAT is recoverable on items which are to be given away as gifts. Whilst they are not for use in the business as such, they are purchases for the business' purpose. However, output tax becomes due at the date of the gift based on the cost to the business. This is primarily an anti-avoidance measure to stop businesses purchasing all manner of things and then giving them away (presumably to themselves!). There is a relaxation for low value items.

Where the cost of the item being given away is no more than £50, input tax claim is available, but there is no output tax. This £50 limit applies to one-off gifts but also to any series of gifts. Thus, if one person is the recipient of several items over time, the limit can be triggered. The limit is to be monitored over a period of twelve months.

Trap. The gift rule applies whenever goods owned by the business are given away. There is no provision here for a charge only to arise when goods are given to customers or other business contacts. The effect of this is that gifts to staff at Christmas or on special occasions such as weddings or retirement are caught.

4.3.3. Business samples

The business gift rules do not apply to genuine commercial samples. It's common for businesses to give away samples of their product to potential customers to demonstrate its quality and characteristics. These often come in a different form to the finished product. For example, manufacturers of beauty products will often create small tester pots as well as the larger volume items to be sold to the public. These are clearly labelled as samples and create no output tax liability when they are given away.

This practice can give the impression that samples must in some way look different to the end product. This is incorrect. There will be industries in which it isn't appropriate or even possible to create a sample of the goods which is not in every way identical to the actual product being promoted. This doesn't mean that a sample can't be given away without a VAT charge. It's sufficient to ensure that all documents make it clear that the item being given away is given as a sample and not simply as a gift.

4.3.4. Temporary transfer of goods

Where goods are taken out of a business temporarily rather than permanently, this creates a supply of services for VAT purposes and VAT becomes due.

EXAMPLE

Olly Orpington runs a landscape gardening business. He has a great deal of gardening and construction equipment as a result. At weekends he uses this equipment to work on his own property but he does not pay his company for this. The assets are being taken out of the business temporarily and so a VAT charge arises. This is quite low as it's calculated on the cost to him of providing the assets. In this case it is limited primarily to minor depreciation, some incidental costs of repair, spare parts and other consumables such as fuel for the mowers.

Trap. For other businesses the costs will be higher. Consider the situation where computers are provided to staff who work from home. This is a clear business purpose giving input tax credit. However, if those computers are also available for private use outside office hours, a significant output tax charge could be created.

4.3.5. Services

Similar rules apply to bought in services which are put to non-business use as apply to goods, but without the £50 relaxation rule.

4.3.6. Cancellation of registration

When a business cancels its registration because it ceases to trade or its turnover falls below the de-registration limit, it will receive a final VAT return. This covers all supplies made and received since the last return to the cancellation date. It will also be necessary to include an output tax charge to reflect the value of goods still owned by the business at that time.

EXAMPLE

Rod Rugby owns and runs a joinery company. As he's winding it down, turnover has decreased to £50k a year. He cancels the company's VAT registration. The company owns a delivery van, woodworking equipment and a small stock of timber. The original cost of the items was £50,000 on which the company reclaimed the VAT. They are now worth £10,000, and so output tax of £2,000 is payable (20% x £10,000) as a result of deregistration.

TIP

When cancelling your registration, you don't have to account for VAT on business goods and assets if the amount of VAT would be no more than £1,000, i.e. the value of the goods etc. doesn't exceed £6,000 including VAT (£5,000 + 20% VAT (£1,000) = £6,000).

4.4. VALUATION OF SUPPLIES

Output tax is due based on the value of the goods or services supplied. The value is normally whatever the parties to the transaction have agreed it to be. There is no requirement for market value to be applied or for a transaction to make a profit. The VATman can only impose such a requirement if the parties are connected and the recipient of the supply can't recover the VAT element as input tax.

The VATman always refers to value before VAT is added, so something valued at £100 gives rise to a £20 VAT charge. The full price paid, £120 is referred to as the consideration.

Note. Consideration includes anything received in payment, not just cash, so it can be the exchange of goods. Also, it doesn't matter whether consideration is received from the customer or someone else - it still counts for VAT. In this way, barter transactions give rise to a VAT charge even though there may be no money changing hands.

EXAMPLE 1

Barry Birmingham a second-hand car dealer bought a used Renault Clio for £4,000. He would normally look to sell it for £5,000, making a VAT inclusive profit of £1,000, giving rise to an output tax charge of £166.67. Instead, he sells it at cost to his friend Bobby Bolton. He makes no profit and so there's no output tax under the second-hand goods scheme. Barry does not have to account for any tax.

EXAMPLE 2

Rupert Ripon has a bicycle in stock that should sell for £1,000. However, it has been in stock for over a year and so he decides to mark it down to £800 and he is able to sell it. The consideration is £800 and VAT of £133.34 is due.

In these examples, the expected sales value is not achieved and output tax due is reduced accordingly.

Trap. Had Rupert sold the bicycle to his son for £10 instead, the connected party rule would allow HMRC to seek VAT based on the normal market value of £1,000 and not the amount received.

4.5.   PLACE OF SUPPLY - THE EFFECT OF OUTPUT TAX

VAT is territorial, meaning that it only applies to supplies of goods and services that take place in the UK. For VAT, but not for other tax purposes, the UK consists of the mainland of England, Scotland and Wales, Northern Ireland, most of the islands around the shores and the twelve-mile territorial waters.

The Isle of Man is strictly not part of the UK for VAT purposes as it has its own VAT law which is almost identical to that of the UK. But because it has a so-called Customs Union with the UK, it's treated as if it was part of the UK for VAT purposes. However, the Channel Islands are outside the UK for VAT purposes.

The rules for determining where a supply takes place for VAT varies for goods and services.

4

4.5.1. Goods

If the goods are in the UK at the time of supply and their supply does not involve them leaving the UK, they are supplied in the UK, and so UK VAT is due at the appropriate rate.

If the goods are outside the UK and are not to come here, then they are supplied outside the UK and no UK VAT is due; the supplies are outside the scope of UK VAT.

Trap. The UK isn't the only country you have to worry about; a UK company exporting goods from one overseas country to another could be within the scope of the VAT law of one or both of those countries. So always seek local tax advice where there's a foreign aspect to your business.

If the supply of the goods involves their removal either to or from the UK, there are special rules for determining whether they take place in the UK (see Chapter 13).

4.5.2. Services

The rules for services are complex and depend on a combination of the type of supply you're making, which country you and the customer belong in and whether you're in business or not (see Chapter 13).

KEY POINTS

- VAT is only chargeable where a tax point is triggered
- there are two types of tax point: "basic" and "actual"
- a basic tax point occurs when goods are delivered or services completed
- actual tax points occur when payment is made or an invoice issued before or shortly after the delivery of goods or completion of services. These override basic tax points
- paying VAT output tax to the VATman can be deferred by manipulation of the tax points
- invoices can be issued up to a year in advance without triggering tax points
- even where there's no sale, certain transactions, such as making a business gift, can trigger a VAT charge
- VAT payable on the value of a supply you make is the amount of cash or value of other consideration, e.g. an exchange of goods you receive, except where the transaction is with a connected party where VAT is instead worked out on the market value.

CHAPTER 5

Input tax

5.1.   WHAT IS INPUT TAX?

Broadly speaking, input tax is the VAT your business incurs on purchases. This is usually relatively easy to identify from the invoice or receipt you receive when you buy something. But just because you pay VAT it doesn't guarantee that you're entitled to reclaim it; there are rules and conditions to be met before you can include input tax on your VAT returns.

5.1.1.   Supply

There has to be a supply of goods or services. If there's no supply, there can't be any VAT to claim.

EXAMPLE

Barry Birmingham orders a new reception desk for his car dealership. The supplier raises a VAT invoice for the new desk but goes into liquidation before it is delivered. There has been no supply of goods or services, so there can be no VAT reclaim, even though Barry holds what appears to be a valid invoice.

5.1.2.   VAT-registered supplier

The supplier of the goods or services must be VAT registered. If the supplier is not registered, VAT can't be shown on an invoice and so be claimable.

5.1.3.   Taxable services or goods

The goods or services supplied must be subject to VAT at a positive rate (standard or reduced rate). If VAT is charged incorrectly on zero-rated or exempt supplies, there is no claim.

Trap. You must be vigilant to ensure that you only pay VAT where it's due, if it isn't then you're not entitled to reclaim it. Where you believe you've been charged VAT incorrectly, you must take up the matter with the supplier, not the VATman.

Sometimes suppliers believe they are protecting themselves from the VATman by charging VAT if they aren't sure whether it's chargeable. But there can be penalties for incorrectly charging VAT.

TIP

The VATman can come to your rescue where you believe you're being charged VAT incorrectly. It's worth contacting the National Advice Service and explaining the situation. While they are not obliged to intervene on your behalf, they often will.

5.2. BUSINESS-RELATED CLAIMS ONLY

5.2.1. Only supplies to a business count

With only a few limited exceptions (see staff expenses below), VAT is claimable on supplies made to your business, not to someone else.

EXAMPLE

George of Glasgow Ltd runs a design consultancy. The company enters into a lease on new offices as a tenant. Part of the deal is that George pays its landlord's legal costs. The landlord instructs solicitors to protect his interests in the lease negotiations. The solicitors are supplying their services to the landlord, not George. The fact that George is paying does not give it the right to recover the VAT element of its bill.

If the building is subject to the option to tax, the landlord is able to recover the VAT, in which case George should only pay the net amount. If the rent is exempt, then George must pay the full invoice amount and suffer irrecoverable VAT.

5.2.2. VAT incurred for the purpose of the business

The supply of goods or services must be for business purposes, as well as being made to the business. Thus, a director might arrange for their company to purchase a new computer for a member of their family. Whilst the supply is made to the company, it's not for the company's business and so it can't claim back the input tax.

TIP

Where there is a dual use, the business has a choice; it can apportion the input tax claim and only claim the business element or it can recover all of the VAT as input tax and then account for output tax on the non-business use each VAT return period.

5.2.3. VAT must be correctly calculated

In addition to ensuring that the correct VAT rate has been applied, the business must check the maths. It's surprisingly common for errors to be made by suppliers, mainly those calculating the VAT manually. Overstated VAT can't be reclaimed; instead, you should ask the supplier for a refund of the excess VAT.

5.2.4. Evidence

Assuming that the business has checked all of the above criteria and is satisfied that they have all been met, input tax can be claimed on the VAT return as long as it holds sufficient evidence, e.g. a VAT receipt or invoice.

5.2.5. Full VAT invoice

For the majority of purchases, the business will need a VAT invoice. This must contain at least the following information to be valid for claiming input tax:

- a sequential number based on one or more series which uniquely identifies the document
- the time of the supply
- the date of the issue of the document
- the name, address and registration number of the supplier
- the name and address of the person to whom the goods or services are supplied
- a description sufficient to identify the goods or services supplied
- for each description, the quantity of the goods or the extent of the services, and the rate of VAT and the amount payable, excluding VAT, expressed in any currency
- the gross total amount payable, excluding VAT, expressed in any currency
- the rate of any cash discount offered
- the total amount of VAT chargeable, expressed in Sterling
- the unit price
- where a margin scheme is applied under s.50A or s.53 of the **Value Added Tax Act 1994**, a relevant reference or any indication that a margin scheme has been applied
- where a VAT invoice relates in whole or part to a supply where the person supplied is liable to pay the tax, a relevant reference or any indication that the supply is one where the customer is liable to pay the tax.

Download Zone

For an **Invoice Checklist**, visit **http://books.indicator.co.uk**. You'll find the access code on page 2 of this book.

5.2.6. Retailers' invoices

Where purchases are made from retailers, i.e. traders whose main business is selling to the public, and the purchase cost is no more than £250, an invoice showing less detail can be used.

The detail required is:

- the name, address and registration number of the retailer
- the time of the supply
- a description sufficient to identify the goods or services supplied
- the total amount payable including VAT; and
- for each rate of VAT chargeable, the gross amount payable including VAT, and the rate applicable.

5.2.7.   The need for original documents

The documents held as evidence should be the originals provided by the supplier. Photocopies and duplicates should be avoided wherever possible. If an invoice is mislaid and the supplier issues a replacement, it should be clearly marked as such.

Some businesses issue invoices electronically. These invoices must comply with the normal content requirements and are valid for input tax claims.

5.3.   IMPORTED GOODS

5.3.1.   Import Form C79

When importing goods into the UK from outside the EU, the VATman levies a VAT charge. This VAT is recoverable as input tax in the normal way. The evidence that the tax has been incurred is a Form C79, which is generated by HMRC and sent to the importing business.

TIP

It's essential that you provide your business's VAT registration details to the import company or agent responsible for the Customs declaration, as this information will be included on Form C79.

TIP

Where you import the goods from another EU country, instead of a Form C79, normal commercial evidence of the transaction and the movement of the goods, e.g. order forms and export documents, will be required (see Chapter 13).

5.4. CLAIMING VAT SHOWN ON EMPLOYEE EXPENSES FORMS

There's an exception to the general rule that to reclaim input VAT, evidence of purchase must be in the name of the business reclaiming it. This is usually the case where your employees incur expenses on the company's behalf.

5.4.1. Car fuel

The most common example of this is car fuel paid for by employees (including directors) in respect of business travel for which they claim a mileage allowance from their employer. Evidence is still required in the form of petrol receipts which should be attached to their expenses claims. The amount of VAT you can reclaim is restricted to the amount of VAT on the fuel element of the claim.

EXAMPLE 1

Percy has a fully expensed company car. All he has to do is put petrol in it. His employer reimburses fuel used on business journeys at 12p per mile. In February Percy drove 1,000 business miles and claimed £120. The business can recover £20 as VAT, as long as there are sufficient petrol receipts to cover this amount.

EXAMPLE 2

Paul does not have a company car at all but uses his own car when he travels for business purposes. The business pays him 40p per mile to reflect his insurance, depreciation and other costs. The fuel element of this mileage rate is 12p per mile. In February he drove 300 business miles and so he also claims £120. The business can claim £6 as input tax.

TIP

You can reclaim the VAT on all fuel paid for by your employees even if it's for private travel, so make sure you make it a company policy that employees provide you with all petrol receipts.

TIP

To make the calculation of the fuel element included in an employee's mileage claim, HMRC publishes an advisory rate which it updates every six months.

Download Zone

For a table of **HMRC Approved Mileage Rates**, visit **http://books.indicator.co.uk**. You'll find the access code on page 2 of this book.

5.4.2. Other staff expenses

VAT can be claimed on staff expenses as long as they are incurred for the purposes of the business. Thus a salesperson staying away for a few days may incur costs on travel, accommodation and meals. The VAT element of these costs can be claimed.

Trap. Invoices/receipts are required even though they may show your employee's name. In addition, the VATman will require confirmation that the expenses were incurred in the course of the business. A diary of who the salesperson visited helps to back this up.

5.4.3. What's the £25 rule?

It's possible to claim some VAT as input tax with no back-up documentation apart from an expenses claim. However, the rules are strict and the range of expense items to which it relates is small.

The cost of the purchase must not exceed £25 and you must be satisfied that the supplier was VAT registered and that the item or service supplied was subject to VAT. It must also have been impossible for you to obtain a VAT invoice or receipt at the time of supply. In practice these rules generally restrict claims to coin operated payments such as:

- public pay telephones
- some car parks
- some tolls
- vending machines.

5.5. VAT ON CARS

The general rule is that you can't reclaim VAT on the cost of a car, whether purchased outright or through a financing arrangement such as hire purchase, but there are some exceptions to the rules:

- you're a car dealer who has purchased the car for resale within twelve months
- the car will be used for hiring out with or without a driver, e.g. a taxi service or car rental company
- it will be used to provide driving instruction
- it's not intended that there will be any private use.

5.5.1. What counts as private use?

Private use involves any trips that are not for the purposes of the business and includes home-to-workplace mileage.

Trap. Proving that there is no private use intention can be very difficult and the VATman is vigilant in this area. He has been known to argue that if a car is covered by an insurance policy that allows private mileage, it must be intended to be used for such.

> **TIP**
>
> A genuine pool car that is parked at the business premises rather than at an employee's home and is not allocated to an individual can qualify for an input tax claim.

> **TIP**
>
> Inserting a clause into your employees' contracts of employment prohibiting private use of a car(s) will strengthen the argument that there is no intention to allow private use.

In all other cases, i.e. where the car is bought by a business that does not carry on one of the qualifying trades and there is private use, no input tax claim is available. This is an absolute block; there is no apportionment available to reflect actual usage; it's an all or nothing situation.

5.5.2. Hire and lease rules

A full input claim is available for those leasing or hiring cars for:

- business purposes only, i.e. with no intention to use privately
- use in hiring out with a driver

- use in the provision of driving instruction
- periods of up to ten days.

In all other circumstances you can reclaim 50% of the VAT you pay on the rental or leasing charge.

Note. If a car is hired to replace one which is normally subject to the 50% restriction, the restriction also applies to the hire car, even if it's hired for up to ten days.

T<small>IP</small>

You don't have to adjust the 50% claimed to account for the non-business of the car. For example, if you drive your company car 10% for business and 90% for private purposes, your company can still claim 50% of the VAT it pays on the rental or leasing costs.

5.5.3. Car accessories

Any accessories and optional extras will be treated in the same way as the car to which they are fitted if they are attached before delivery. If they are fitted later, VAT recovery is available as long as it's fitted for business use even if there's some private use.

5.5.4. Repairs and servicing

VAT is recoverable on repair and servicing costs as long as the supply is made to the business, the business bears the cost and there is some business use of the car.

T<small>IP</small>

It doesn't matter whether your business owns the car or not; if the cost of repairs or servicing is incurred by your business it can reclaim 100% of the VAT it pays as long as there's some business use of the car, even where it's just, say, 5%.

T<small>IP</small>

Some hire or lease contracts include a maintenance element. The VAT on this can be reclaimed in full even where the VAT reclaimable on the rental/lease charge is restricted to 50% (see above).

5.6. BUSINESS AND STAFF ENTERTAINMENT

VAT regulations block the recovery of input tax incurred in relation to business entertaining. The rules are very broad and include all forms of entertaining of suppliers, customers and other business contacts. Both revenue and capital costs are covered, e.g. paying for a meal (a revenue cost) or purchasing a yacht for use in entertaining (a capital cost). The exclusion to these provisions is where the entertaining is provided to an overseas customer or their representative.

For these purposes, a prospective customer is counted as a customer. The VATman has had this rule forced on him by Europe and so he seeks to impose some restrictions. He will argue against deduction where he feels that the costs are not necessary expenditure or are excessive in amount or nature. Providing a customer with a sandwich at a meeting will always be acceptable, but taking one to Ascot with no expense spared will be queried. Be prepared to justify any claims.

TIP

The block doesn't extend to costs incurred in entertaining staff so, for example, you can reclaim VAT on the cost of your Christmas party or any other function.

Trap. Where your staff attend a business entertainment function that is primarily for other purposes, e.g. to entertain your customers, you can't reclaim the proportion of VAT on the costs relating to your staff.

EXAMPLE

Walter Walsingham has an estate agency business. He runs three events each year.

Once a year he treats his staff to a day out in London. Walter pays for the whole day, transport, meals, drinks, theatre trip and overnight stay. As the entertainment is purely for his staff, he is entitled to full input tax recovery.

In the summer Walter runs a golf day for clients and contacts. The object of the day is to entertain those guests. No input tax recovery is available even though most of his staff attend as well. The staff are there primarily to keep the guests happy and so their attendance is seen as incidental.

At Christmas Walter hosts a party for his staff and invites them to bring along a guest if they would like to. The purpose of the event is to reward the employees for their hard work during the year and so input tax recovery is available. However, as there are non-employees present (the guests) the entertaining block applies as well. The input tax is apportioned to reflect this and only the element of VAT incurred that relates to staff is recovered. This is usually done on a head-count basis but any reasonable method can be used.

5.7.   RECLAIMING PRE-REGISTRATION INPUT TAX

It's common for businesses to trade for some time before becoming VAT registered. Whilst trading in this pre-registration period the business will incur VAT on costs and cannot recover it, as it doesn't have a VAT return upon which to do so.

When it registers, the business is entitled to recover some of this tax.

5.7.1.   Goods

The business can recover VAT on goods incurred up to four years prior to the date of registration as long as the goods are still owned at the time. This includes stock items as well as capital assets of the business.

As with all purchases, invoices are required to back up the claim.

5.7.2.   Services

VAT incurred on services in the six months prior to the effective date of registration can also be recovered.

Claims for pre-registration are to be made on the business' first VAT return.

TIP

As a concession, businesses wishing to take advantage of the 1% rate discount available under the flat rate scheme by adopting it from the date of registration, can recover pre-registration input tax on their first VAT return. They can do this even though input tax claims are not normally available under the scheme.

5.8.   RECLAIMING POST-DEREGISTRATION INPUT TAX

After a business ceases to be VAT registered, it will no longer receive VAT returns upon which to claim input tax. However, it may still incur costs which relate to the period in which it was registered. Commonly this will be restricted to items such as accountancy fees for producing accounts relating to the previous year's trading or legal fees in selling the business. This tax is recoverable and can be claimed using Form VAT 427, which should be submitted to HMRC within six months of cancellation of the registration.

KEY POINTS

- input tax is the VAT paid on purchases
- you can't reclaim input tax unless the purchase is made for business purposes and VAT has been correctly charged
- VAT charged on imported goods can be reclaimed subject to the same rules as VAT on UK purchases
- VAT on the cost of cars is blocked even where they are used for your business, but there are some exceptions, e.g. cars bought for resale by dealers, those used as taxis or for renting out
- you can reclaim 50% of the VAT on car lease or rental costs
- input VAT can be reclaimed on the cost of staff entertainment but not other business entertainment
- subject to restrictions, you can reclaim VAT on costs incurred before you register and after you deregister.

CHAPTER 6

Returns

6.1. INTRODUCTION

Once registered for VAT, every business is required to submit periodic returns to HMRC declaring the amount of tax payable or refund due to them. The VAT return asks for relatively little detail compared to, say, a Corporation Tax return, consisting of only nine boxes for the entry of data. Care is required to ensure that these returns are completed accurately and that they are submitted in good time along with any payment required. There are harsh penalties for mistakes and lateness in either submission or payment.

6.2. RETURN PERIODS

6.2.1. Quarterly VAT periods

Most businesses will submit returns covering periods of three months. These are arranged in what are referred to as the VAT staggers, as follows:

STAGGER	PERIODS ENDING
Stagger one	March, June, September, December
Stagger two	April, July, October, January
Stagger three	May, August, November, February

TIP

You can ask the VATman to change the VAT stagger to your advantage. For example, where you have a seasonal trade biased around summer trade, you might benefit from Stagger three so that the VAT you collect on sales in your high season - June/July/August - won't be payable to the VATman until you send in your VAT return for the August quarter, i.e. not until the end of September.

6.2.2. Annual VAT returns

Some businesses opt to use annual accounting, which requires the submission of a return each year under the annual accounting scheme (see Chapter 3).

6.2.3. Monthly returns

You can ask the VATman to send you returns each month.

TIP

Monthly returns will improve your cash flow where your business's input tax regularly exceeds the output tax, meaning that you'll be entitled to a regular VAT refund. However, the downside of the arrangement is the administrative burden of having to complete monthly forms.

6.3. SECURITY PAYMENTS

Another reason for adopting monthly rather than quarterly returns is to reduce the cost where HMRC requires a security payment from your business. If the VATman suspects that your business is or may soon become insolvent and so unable to pay its debts, including its VAT liability, it can, subject to conditions, ask your company to make a security payment.

Trap. If you've been involved in a failed business, even though it may not have been any fault of yours, the VATman might be nervous that the same thing will happen again. As a result, he has the power to require a security deposit from your current business. This will be based on the amount of VAT which could be lost.

For quarterly returns the security is based on six months of VAT liability.

TIP

If you're required to make a security payment, by opting for monthly returns the amount reduces to four months' VAT.

TIP

You can appeal against the VATman's request for a securtity payment if you believe it's unfair. See Appendix 3 for details of when and how to make an appeal.

6.4. PAYMENTS ON ACCOUNT

The payment on account system is designed to aid government cash flow. In ordinary circumstances a business may receive output tax from its customers up to four months before it has to pay it over to HMRC. This cash flow advantage for the business is a cash flow cost for the Treasury. In order to redress this, companies who are liable to pay a large amount of VAT are required to pay monthly, although quarterly returns usually still apply.

A business with VAT payments due to HMRC in excess of £2 million per annum is required to pay monthly. This tax due figure includes quarterly VAT payment on returns and also any other payments that are required to be made to HMRC.

Note. The £2 million limit includes VAT payable when you import goods and services. It's easy to overlook this, which could mean you miss switching to monthly payments at the right time resulting in penalties.

6.5. WHAT ARE SPECIAL ACCOUNTING PERIODS?

Many businesses prefer to run their accounting records to the end of a trading week rather than to a fixed calendar month-end. This can lead to complex adjustments being required if the business is on standard return period dates which do not coincide.

TIP

If your business operates in this way, perhaps approximating months using a four-week reporting schedule, you can ask for special VAT returns to align with your accounting periods. You'll need to contact HMRC at the beginning of each year detailing your accounting schedule.

6.6. DEADLINES

All VAT registered businesses are now required to submit returns online and the deadline is the 7th of the month after the month following the period-end. Thus, a return running to March 31 must be filed by May 7. Any VAT due is also payable online and the funds must be cleared in the VATman's account by this deadline.

6.6.1. Using estimates

Where you don't have accurate figures for your VAT return, it's better to submit it showing the best estimates you can make rather than delaying a return and potentially running up penalties and surcharges.

Note. Where you intend to use an estimate of a material value, you should contact the VATman for approval first. Permission will not be given on a regular basis but it still represents a useful concession. You can then correct the figures either by adjusting a later return, where the difference is less than £10,000 or, where the adjustment needed is greater than this, notify the VATman by letter or on Form 652 of the reason for and amount of the correction.

6.6.2.   Asking for time to pay

Where your business doesn't have sufficient funds to meet its VAT bill, it's possible to agree time to pay with the VATman.

TIP

Don't leave your request for time to pay until after payment is due. Contact the VATman in advance and you'll stand a much better chance of success.

6.7.   VAT RETURN BOXES

There are only nine boxes requiring data input on the VAT return (and online it calculates two of them for you).

- **Box 1 - output tax.** This is the total output tax due to HMRC in the period on supplies made with a tax point within the period. It also includes output tax on any deemed supplies, reverse charge supplies and adjustments.
- **Box 2 - acquisition tax.** VAT due on goods purchased from VAT-registered suppliers from other EU states (see Chapter 13).
- **Box 3 - output tax due.** The total of the amounts declared in Boxes 1 and 2.
- **Box 4 - input tax.** All input tax claimed in the period on purchases and imports. Also, any VAT declared on reverse charge services and in Box 2 can be claimed here, subject to any partial exemption or other blocks. Any input tax adjustments from prior periods will also be included here (subject to the disclosure limits).
- **Box 5 - net tax due or repayable.** The difference between Boxes 4 and 5. Where output tax exceeds input tax, the business must make payment to HRMC. Where input tax exceeds output tax, the VATman will pay the tax directly into the business' bank account.
- **Box 6 - turnover.** The net value of income in the period excluding items that are outside the scope of VAT by virtue of being non-business.
- **Box 7 - expenditure.** The net value of expenditure in the period excluding items that are outside the scope of VAT by virtue of being non-business.
- **Box 8 - EC sales of goods.** The value of goods sold to EU customers which have been zero-rated under the despatch rules (see Chapter 13).
- **Box 9 - EC purchases of goods.** The value of goods purchased from EU suppliers which have been zero-rated under the acquisition rules (see Chapter 13).

Download Zone

For a **VAT Return Checklist**, visit **http://books.indicator.co.uk**. You'll find the access code on page 2 of this book.

6.8.   ERROR CORRECTION

If a business discovers that it has made a mistake on a VAT return, there are special rules on how to go about correcting it.

6.8.1.   Time limit

Errors made within the previous four years can be corrected. Anything prior to that period can be left alone. This can be good news if the errors found were in your favour but bad news when it's the other way around.

Note. The four-year period runs from the end of the VAT return period in which the error was made (for output tax) or the due date for submission of the return (for input tax).

6.8.2.   Monetary limits

Small errors can be amended on the current VAT return. Larger errors are to be disclosed separately to HMRC.

The limit for error correction on a return is the greater of:

- £10,000; and
- 1% of current period Box 6 turnover.

The 1% test is capped at £50,000 to stop very large businesses having enormous materiality limits.

6.8.3.   It's the net error which counts

EXAMPLE

Helen Harrogate finds that she has missed a month's takings off her 03/11 VAT return. The output tax that should have been declared was £12,000. She also finds that over the past four years she has been incorrectly accounting for output tax on some of the girls clothing sold through the shop. These sales should have been zero-rated. She finds that the output tax overpaid amounts to £4,000. The net error is £8,000 and so she is entitled to adjust the net amount on her current VAT return period.

Had she only found the first error, she would have been required to disclose separately.

6.8.4. Form VAT 652

When disclosing errors, Form VAT 652 should be used. If preferred, you can provide the information via a letter, but take care to include:

- the nature of the errors
- an explanation as to how they arose; and
- the amounts involved by VAT return period.

Trap. Correcting an error on a VAT return does not count as disclosure for penalty purposes. You must note that an error has been corrected in your VAT return workings and so it will be obvious to any VAT officer visiting at a later date. If they feel that the error arose through carelessness or was deliberate, they may assess a penalty, and the scope for reducing this will be significantly less because you didn't disclose it.

EXAMPLE

Helen adjusts the £8,000 net error she found on her VAT return. HMRC finds the error correction on its next visit and concludes that missing a month's takings off a return is careless. A 30% penalty is imposed.

If Helen had disclosed the error to the VATman when she found it, the disclosure would mean that no penalty would be charged.

TIP

Make it extremely clear to the VATman that you are disclosing for penalty purposes but that you have adjusted your return. If you don't do this, the VATman will assume that the return has not been adjusted and will assess for the tax, so you could end up paying twice!

KEY POINTS

- VAT returns are usually required quarterly
- you can apply to the VATman for monthly returns; this will be of benefit where you usually receive VAT refunds
- most VAT-registered businesses are required to submit returns online
- you're allowed an extra seven days to submit and pay your VAT bill where you file and pay online
- you can use estimated figures on your VAT returns where you have prior permission from the VATman
- you can correct errors of up to £10,000 in total on one VAT return by adjusting a later return, but to reduce the risk of penalties you should tell the VATman separately that you have done this.

CHAPTER 7

Capital goods scheme

7.1. INTRODUCTION

For the majority of purchases you make for your business you only have to think about claiming input tax at the time of purchase. Once you've reclaimed it that's the end of the matter. For example, if you buy a new van, you can recover the VAT paid as input tax. If you later use the van for private use, you could be liable to pay some output tax but input tax doesn't need to be recalculated. Therefore, if an asset starts life intended for making VATable supplies, there's no adjustment if you later use it to make exempt supplies. But there are exceptions.

The VATman recognises that this might give your business an unfair advantage, so he invented the capital goods scheme (CGS). This requires businesses to make adjustments to input tax they've claimed where the use of certain assets changes.

7.2. WHAT ASSETS ARE AFFECTED BY THE CGS?

7.2.1. Computers

Individual purchases of computer hardware (not software) where the cost to the business is £50,000 or more (excluding VAT).

Note. This applies to individual pieces of hardware.

> **TIP**
>
> You can reclaim the full amount of VAT paid on the purchase of computer hardware even where the cost exceeds £50,000, provided that no single item exceeds this limit.

Trap. The cost of delivery and installation etc. counts towards the CGS limit.

7.2.2. Aircraft, ships, boats and other vessels

Again, there is a £50,000 limit. Purchases below the limit are not caught by the scheme, those above are. Also included are the manufacture, refurbishment, fitting out, alteration and extension of such assets if the cost of doing so exceeds £50,000.

7.2.3. Land and buildings

• buildings and parts of buildings where there is a change from VATable to non-VATable use

- purchases of land, buildings and civil engineering work (freehold or leasehold)

- construction of a building or civil engineering work

- alteration or extension of a building which results in at least 10% increased floor space

- refurbishment or fitting out of a building.

For land and buildings the CGS is only triggered where the amount paid for the work or assets is both subject to VAT and at least £250,000 (excluding VAT).

For example, a business paying a lease premium of £300,000 is within the scheme. One paying £240,000 is not. A business purchasing a new web server for £60,000 is within the scheme, another purchasing a new office network for £75,000 is not if this is made up of many individual items each valued at less than £50,000.

7.3.   INPUT TAX ON CAPITAL GOODS ASSETS

Usually, a fully taxable business, i.e. one that doesn't make exempt supplies, will recover all the VAT on the item. But where the asset is to be used exclusively in making exempt supplies, you can't reclaim any of the VAT. For an asset purchased to make both taxable and exempt supplies, a proportion will be recovered based on the business' partial exemption method (see Chapter 8). However, different rules apply to assets within the CGS.

Trap. Unlike other assets, adjustments to the amount of input tax you claimed at the time of purchase can be necessary for assets in CGS.

7.4.   ADJUSTMENT PERIODS

There are set times when you must review the amount of input tax reclaimed on assets within the CGS. For computer hardware, there are five "adjustment periods"; for land and buildings there are ten, unless the asset is a lease with less than ten years to run in which case there are five adjustment periods.

At the end of each adjustment period, coinciding with the business' VAT year-end - usually March 31, April 30 or May 31, you must consider how the asset has been used. If it has been different from the original use, an adjustment may be required.

> **TIP**
>
> You can reclaim further VAT input tax where the use of a CGS asset to make taxable supplies has increased during an adjust-ment period.

Immie Immingham's finance company is partially exempt supplying loan finance to both UK and non-EU associates. The interest received from the UK subsidiaries is exempt from VAT, that from the non-EU companies outside the scope of VAT but with input tax credit. The company buys a new office block in 2011 from which to trade. The building costs £1,000,000 plus VAT of £200,000. In the VAT year 2011/12 income is 60% UK and 40% non-EU.

Immie Finance recovers £80,000 being 40% of the VAT incurred.

In the year 2012/13 UK interest income has dropped as a loan has been repaid. The income split is now 50:50.

Immie Finance makes a CGS adjustment to reflect this. The original recovery was 40% and the use in the current adjustment period was 50%. A further 10% recovery is available. This 10% claim is calculated by applying it to 10% of the original tax incurred (20% for computers). In this way Immie Finance recovers a further £2,000 (original tax of £200,000/10 = £20,000 x 10% = £2,000).

In the year 2013/14, UK interest increases dramatically due to a large acquisition. UK interest rises to 80%. Immie Finance repays £4,000 (original tax £200,000/10 = £20,000 x 20% (the difference between original recovery of 40% and current period recovery of 20%)).

7.4.1.   When to make CGS adjustments

Adjustments are made on the second VAT return following the VAT year-end; thus a business with calendar quarter returns will have a March 31 VAT year-end and any adjustments will be included on the September return.

7.4.2.   Adjustments on selling an asset

If a CGS item is sold before all of the adjustment periods have elapsed, special rules apply. An adjustment is made to cover the period from the beginning of the current adjustment period to the date of disposal, usually resulting in a short adjustment period. Any remaining adjustments to bring the total to five or ten are also made when an asset is sold or disposed of in another way, e.g. taken out of the business.

Where an item is disposed of as a taxable supply (computers, new freehold commercial property or land and buildings subject to the option to tax), it's treated as being used for fully taxable purposes for any remaining periods. If it's disposed of on an exempt basis, then the use for the remaining periods is 100% exempt.

EXAMPLE

Immie Finance sells its office building after seven complete adjustment periods. She opts to tax and charges VAT on the sale. The asset is treated as fully taxable for the remaining three adjustment periods. Immie Finance claims a further repayment of £36,000 (original tax £200,000/10 = £20,000 x 60% (difference between original claim of 40% and current use 100%) = £12,000 x 3 (three remaining adjustment periods) = £36,000).

TIP

Opting to make a property VATable can save you tax. In this example, opting to charge VAT on the building is key. If the option were not taken, the disposal would be exempt and the remaining adjustment periods would have a 0% recovery rate. Immie Finance would have to repay £24,000 of the VAT it has reclaimed to HMRC.

7.5. ANTI-AVOIDANCE

As an anti-avoidance measure, a business disposing of an asset within the CGS period may not recover more input tax than output tax accounted for. This rule is intended to stop businesses creating artificial low value supplies on which they charge VAT just so they can reclaim a greater amount of input VAT.

TIP

If you're selling an item at a loss or a low value for genuine commercial reasons, such as poor market conditions, ordinary depreciation etc., you can ask the VATman to waive the anti-avoidance rules. Just write to him and explain the circumstances in which the low value sale is being made.

7.6. SHORT CGS PERIODS

Where an asset is disposed of as part of a transfer of a going concern (TOGC) (see Chapter 9) or your business enters or leaves a VAT group, any CGS periods come to an end at that date. In this way not all CGS adjustment periods will be of twelve months' duration.

Where the asset forms part of a TOGC, the new owner becomes liable for any remaining adjustment periods. The vendor must provide sufficient data to the purchaser to allow this to happen, including:

- the original tax incurred

- the original recovery percentage

- details of how many adjustment periods are still outstanding.

Following these short periods, further adjustment periods revert to being twelve months' long but start from that date.

EXAMPLE

Adrian Aberdeen sells one of his commercial properties on July 31 2011 as a TOGC. It cost him £300,000 plus VAT in 2008 and so is still within the scheme; he has undertaken three adjustment calculations so far and has calendar quarter returns. Adrian makes an adjustment for the period April 1 to July 31. His purchaser, Suzanne Salcombe, becomes liable for the remaining adjustment periods which will run from August 1 to July 31 each year.

KEY POINTS

- the capital goods scheme (CGS) applies to purchases of single items of computer hardware, ships, boats and aircraft costing more than £50,000 and and buildings costing more than £250,000
- VAT can be reclaimed at the time of purchase of CGS assets in line with the normal rules
- the use of the CGS asset must be reviewed at the end of each VAT year
- where the proportion of your taxable supplies increases from one year to the next, more of the VAT paid on the purchase of the CGS asset can be reclaimed
- where the proportion of taxable supplies reduces from one year to the next, some of the VAT originally reclaimed must be repaid.

CHAPTER 8

Partial exemption

8.1. INTRODUCTION

Partial exemption is simply about how much VAT you can reclaim on purchases. Chapter 5 looked at the rules relating to recovery of VAT, but didn't dwell on one important restriction.

VAT is recoverable only where all of the basic requirements are met, but there's one further crucial criterion to be satisfied: VAT is only recoverable in full if it results in a VATable supply. In other words, if a business makes supplies which are subject to VAT at the standard, reduced or zero rates, VAT input tax can be reclaimed on the purchases it makes in relation to these. But where a business makes only exempt supplies, it can't reclaim any VAT; in fact, it can't even register for VAT.

The partial exemption rules apply where your business has a mixture of taxable and exempt supplies. You can recover the input tax in full where it relates to a taxable supply, but not where it corresponds to the exempt supplies. In between sit the partial exemption rules which are there to apportion VAT on purchases which you use to make both taxable and exempt supplies. This is called "residual VAT". Typically, this will be overheads, such as rent, telephone, professional fees, etc.

8.2. ATTRIBUTION OF INPUT TAX

The first thing you need to do is attribute input tax to taxable and exempt supplies, i.e. work out whether the cost of a purchase is used exclusively for either a taxable supply or an exempt one.

- VAT attributable to taxable supplies is fully recoverable in the normal way
- VAT relating to exempt supplies can't be recovered at all unless it's within the de minimis limit (see below)
- VAT on the remaining purchases is then apportioned to allow some recovery.

Tip

Attribution is done on a purchase-by-purchase basis, so, it's vital for partially exempt businesses to set up their bookkeeping systems so that purchases relating to exempt and taxable supplies are attributed correctly. This gives rise to some planning potential.

Example

Adrian Aberdeen has expanded his property portfolio. He now has seven commercial buildings and 18 residential properties. He has opted to tax all of the commercial properties and charges VAT on the rent. He employs Archie to carry out routine maintenance and repair on the buildings for him.

In March, Archie charges him £2,000 plus VAT (£400) for work done on the residential property and £150 plus VAT (£30) for the commercial units. If Archie sends separate invoices for each property, the £400 relating to the residential units will not be recoverable as it relates wholly to exempt income (residential rental). If, however, Adrian asks him to raise only one invoice showing the full VAT of £430, it can't be attributed exclusively to either taxable or exempt income and so is included in the partial exemption apportionment. More input tax will be recoverable as a result. Working with suppliers in this way can result in significant savings.

8.3. RESIDUAL VAT - PARTIAL EXEMPTION STANDARD METHOD

Following the attribution exercise, the input tax on the remaining purchases will need to be apportioned to reflect the relative amount used in the making of taxable supplies. Most businesses use what's known as the "standard method", though many other methods can be used.

The standard method splits the VAT on un-attributed purchases using the ratio of taxable to non-taxable income.

EXAMPLE

In the year to March 31 2011, Adrian Aberdeen has seven commercial properties that he rents out, giving him £212,000 of taxable income each year. His 18 residential properties produce £86,400 per annum. His total income is therefore £298,400. Taxable income represents 71.04% of this. Adrian is entitled to recover 72% of his residual input tax.

TIP

The recoverable percentage is rounded up in the business' favour unless residual input tax exceeds £400,000 per month, in which case two decimal places are to be used.

8.3.1. Must all income be included in the calculation?

When working out the taxable income percentage there are some income items that must be left out:

- sales of capital assets, e.g. machinery used to produce the goods you sell. Including these would distort the partial exemption calculation
- incidental income - this could be a small amount of bank interest or occasional rental income. Where exempt financial or property income is received, it can be ignored if it's incidental to the main business activity and isn't a product of the business in its own right.

- overseas income - most income received from non-UK sources will be outside the scope of UK VAT.

EXAMPLE

Lionel Leighton has UK taxable turnover of £1.3m. He also supplies design services to EU businesses and generates a further £500k from this. He has exempt rental income of £200k from a portfolio of buy-to-lets. As the EU income would bear UK VAT if supplied within the UK, it counts in his partial exemption calculation as if it were taxable income. He can thus recover 90% of residual tax (£1.3m + £500k/£2m).

8.3.2.   How many calculations?

The standard method offers some flexibility. You can carry out a separate calculation each VAT return period with an annual adjustment, or use the previous year's percentage on a provisional basis throughout the year and carry out an annual adjustment calculation after the year has ended.

Trap. Quarterly calculations are arguably more accurate but mean more work; annual-only calculations result in less work but can lead to large adjustments if the business is changing.

EXAMPLE

Adrian's income is relatively uniform throughout the year so he opts to use one year's percentage on a provisional basis for the next. Using the figures from the previous example, he recovers 72% of his residual input tax for the VAT returns in the year ending March 31 2012. He then carries out one calculation and finds that in the year his income was only slightly different. He had a vacant period in two of his flats and had an increase in rent on one of the commercial properties following a rent review. Income was £218,000 taxable and £84,500 exempt.

Total income was thus £302,500 of which taxable income was 72.06%. His recovery rate for the year is 73% (after rounding). He can then revisit the recoveries in the individual return periods and recover a little more.

He finds that he recovered £8,640 in the year (residual tax of £12,000 x 72%). His recoverable tax was residual tax of £12,000 x 73%, £8,760, meaning that a further £120 can be now claimed.

8.4.   WORKING OUT THE ANNUAL ADJUSTMENT

This annual adjustment is to be done after each VAT year. A business's VAT year runs to March 31, April 30 or May 30 depending upon VAT quarterly periods. If your business's financial year runs to a different date, e.g. December 31, you can ask the VATman to align the VAT year with this. This can save administration.

TIP

The adjustment following an annual partial exemption calculation can be included on the last return for the year or you can opt to delay it until the first return of the next year. Where you're claiming back more VAT, make the adjustment in the earlier return, but where the adjustment means more VAT payable, delay it until the later one.

8.5.   DE MINIMIS LIMITS FOR PARTIAL EXEMPTION

A further important VAT break exists where your business has relatively low levels of exempt input tax. In this case the rules allow you to reclaim VAT paid on purchases where these relate to exempt supplies.

There are two ways to calculate the "de minimis" limit. The first requires you to make the full partial exemption calculation and then apply the test, while the second allows you to carry out less detailed workings.

8.5.1.   Full calculation

First, you must carry out the attribution exercise, see above, and then the residual tax apportionment. This will show the recoverable input VAT, and that which relates to your exempt activity. If the exempt amount of input tax is less than: **(1)** £625 per month on average over the VAT return period; and **(2)** 50% of total input tax, then the business will be classed as de minimis.

Where your business is de minimis, you can reclaim the input tax on all your purchases. The de minimis test must be applied each time a partial exemption calculation is carried out, i.e. quarterly or annually.

Note. The monetary limit of £625 is on average per month. This gives VAT of £1,875 per quarter, £7,500 per annum.

8.5.2. Less detailed calculation

A business is also de minimis, and so can recover all input tax without the full calculation, if either:

- total input tax is less than £625 per month on average; and
- exempt income is less than 50% of total income

or

- total input tax less tax directly attributable to taxable supplies is less than £625 per month on average; and
- exempt income is less than 50% of total income.

TIP

A timing advantage. Where your business is de minimis and has a turnover of less than £1 million in one year, it can treat itself as de minimis for the next, but it must carry out the annual adjustment calculation. Where you expect the amount of VAT you can recover on partially exempt purchases to decrease from one year to the next, using the de minimis assumption means you'll be delaying payment of VAT by up to a year.

8.6. SPECIAL PARTIAL EXEMPTION METHODS

Some businesses will find that splitting residual input tax on an income basis does not give a fair result. Where the cost of generating taxable and exempt income is the same, the standard method will give a reasonable and fair result for the amount of input VAT you can reclaim. However, if, for example, it costs you proportionately more to create taxable income, using the standard method could leave you out of pocket.

TIP

Where you feel that the standard method is not fair, you can ask the VATman to approve any other method you come up with as long as it can demonstrate that this will give a fair result.

Below are some of the non-standard methods of calculating the VAT reclaimable which the VATman has approved:

- the values of inputs attributable to purchases
- the values of inputs attributable to taxable income compared to exempt income
- a transaction count, i.e. the number of taxable and exempt deals rather than their values - this is commonly used in the financial sector or where your income is produced by commission
- floor area used in generating different types of income - common in property businesses and casinos
- staff numbers working in different parts of the business
- internal accounting systems such as monthly management accounts.

Whatever sensible basis put forward will be considered by HMRC.

TIP

You can have different recovery methods for different parts of a business, e.g. different companies in a VAT group. Or you can form a VAT group (see Chapter 1), so that wholly exempt companies within the group can benefit from the taxable supplies made by others.

8.6.1. Other considerations

Special methods can be more complicated than the standard method and:

- require additional analysis of data work
- take longer to carry out and so cost more
- are harder to explain when training new staff
- are harder to check, meaning that VAT officers spend longer in your offices
- are more prone to error due to this complexity.

Nevertheless, they can result in significant savings and so are well worth considering.

Trap. The rounding of recoverable percentages in favour of your business, which is allowed in the standard method, is not normally permitted in a special method. You must use the percentage correct to two decimal places.

Note. Direct attribution will always be the starting point and the recovery method applied to any residual VAT only. It will not be possible to agree a special method with the VATman which doesn't include direct attribution as a first step.

8.6.2. First-year relaxation

For the first year in which a business becomes partially exempt, the standard method may not be appropriate as income streams may not have settled into their long-term pattern and so recoveries based on income can be unfair.

TIP

You could use a special method that suits the purchasing and selling pattern of your business for the first year and then revert to the standard method later. In this situation relaxation of the rules is available without the need for formal agreement with the VATman.

In the first year you can calculate recoverable input tax based on the use to which costs are put, rather than by reference to whether the income you receive is from exempt or taxable supplies. The standard income-based method is then applied after the first year unless a special method is formally approved.

EXAMPLE

Builder Peter Polperrow decides to set up a new development company. The company negotiates the purchase of a plot of land upon which stands a public house. The pub comprises a ground floor bar area, a first floor meeting room suite and a flat on top. Peter plans to convert the bar area and meeting room suite into two flats and refurbish the existing flat. His income from the two new flats will be zero-rated but that from the refurbished unit will be exempt. Peter's new company will be partly exempt. From acquiring the site to completing the works and selling the flats, 14 months elapse. The company has no income in this period and so it would be impossible to use the standard method. Peter is entitled to adopt a use-based approach for this period. He decides to recover based on a floor area system.

8.7. PAYBACK AND CLAWBACK

After you've carried out the attribution exercise you'll be able to identify those purchases which have already been used to make supplies and those which are yet to be used. Where VAT is attributed to future supplies, it's treated as provisional. This means that if you change your intention and make an exempt supply where you originally attributed it to a taxable supply, or vice versa, you'll have to adjust for this in a later VAT return.

Example 1

Peter's company acquires its new site with the pub on it. It incurs VAT on the professional fees associated with the purchase and on architects and other costs in obtaining planning permission. He recovers two-thirds of the VAT under his floor-based apportionment as relating to the two new flats. However, before he commences work, he is offered significantly more for the plot than he paid for it and he accepts the offer. He sells the site as an exempt disposal (he has not opted to tax). The VAT previously recovered was done so as there was an intention to make taxable supplies. The exempt disposal has taken place before those taxable supplies were made, and so the recovery must be revisited and the input tax repaid to HMRC.

The rules operate the other way as well. It may be that Peter finds that the building is in fact unstable and so he applies for revised planning consent to demolish it and redevelop the site instead. He has recovered two-thirds of the VAT on the assumption that an exempt disposal will be made of the old flat once it has been refurbished. Now that the building is to be demolished, that exempt supply will no longer be made. All of the sales will be of new flats and so zero-rated. Full recovery is now available and Peter can go back and claim the VAT previously blocked.

The rules are considered over a six-year period. If a business attributes input tax to one type of intended supply and instead makes another type of supply within six years, an adjustment is needed.

The VATman accepts that sometimes a change of intention is forced on a business by market conditions and may only be temporary. In this situation he may accept an adjustment instead of a reversal of previous treatment.

Example 2

Peter now has permission to demolish the pub and replace it with new flats. He recovers all of the input tax incurred on the basis it will relate to the zero-rated sale of the property he intends to make. However, once he has completed the flats, he finds that the housing market is flat and he can't sell them. His bank is pressing for some repayment on the loans and so he decides to put them on the rental market for six months and then seek to sell again. His original intention to make zero-rated sales has been delayed and exempt supplies are being made instead.

As there is still an intention to makes zero-rated sales, the VATman will allow Peter to repay only part of the VAT involved. This will normally be calculated on a time basis, using a ten-year reference period. Therefore, as Peter intends to rent for only six months, this represents 5% of the ten-year period. Peter would be required to repay only 5% of the VAT originally claimed.

KEY POINTS

- VAT paid on purchases used to make exempt supplies can't be reclaimed unless it's within the de minimis limits
- VAT paid on purchases used to make both taxable and exempt supplies is called "residual VAT"
- where input VAT relating to your exempt supplies exceeds the de minimis limits, you can reclaim a proportion of it where your business makes some taxable supplies
- the standard method for working out the proportion of residual VAT which can be reclaimed is the value of your taxable supplies compared to exempt supplies
- you can create your own formula for working out the amount of reclaimable residual VAT; these are called "special methods"
- special methods must be agreed with the VATman before you can use them except in the first year of business where no permission is required.

CHAPTER 9

Selling or buying a business as a going concern

9.1.   INTRODUCTION

The transfer of going concern provisions (usually shortened to TOGC) are a useful relaxation to the rules, removing the VAT charge from certain sales of business assets.

In ordinary trading a business may purchase an asset, e.g. a new van, and it recovers the VAT element of the purchase price. Some time later the business trades the van in for a new one and is required to account for VAT output tax on the disposal.

The VATman recognises that if a business is selling not just an odd asset but its whole business, the amounts of VAT at stake could be considerable and so hamper the normal commercial consideration. A person purchasing a business rather than starting their own from scratch would have to fund potentially large amounts of VAT prior to submission of the first VAT return.

The flip side is that the VATman is worried that being in receipt of a significantly greater amount of tax than usual might tempt the vendor to hold onto it for longer than they should do.

The TOGC rules get around these issues by laying down certain criteria which, if met, mean no VAT is chargeable on the sale of all or part of a business.

9.2.   TOGC BENEFITS AND PITFALLS

The benefits of TOGC treatment accrue almost exclusively to the purchaser. As far as the vendor of the business is concerned it's just another process to deal with. The difficulty for the vendor is in ensuring that the correct treatment is applied. If VAT is not charged, on the mistaken understanding that the TOGC rules apply, the VATman could assess for VAT and penalties which might not be recoverable from the purchaser.

For the purchaser, making the purchase of a TOGC removes the VAT charge, which is beneficial for funding and avoids any problems with partial exemption. Further, if land and buildings are included in the transfer, a Stamp Duty Land Tax saving can be achieved in certain circumstances (see below).

9.3.   WHEN DOES A TOGC APPLY?

For there to be a VAT-free TOGC, certain conditions must apply.

9.3.1. Going concern

There must be a transfer of assets as a going concern. This doesn't necessarily mean that the business being sold has to be highly profitable, merely that a business is being run using those assets. As long as you are open for business, you can have a TOGC.

9.3.2. Same kind of business

The assets being transferred must be used by the purchaser to carry on the same kind of business as the vendor.

EXAMPLE

Dan Dover sells his sandwich shop business to Phoebe Fishguard who continues to operate the business seamlessly, selling sandwiches from the same premises with the same staff and opening hours. This can be a TOGC.

Trap. A shop doesn't constitute a type of trade in itself. It's the nature of the business that counts.

EXAMPLE

Rupert Ripon sells his cycle shop to Tim Tenby. Tim closes the shop for two weeks whilst he converts the property and reopens as a branch of his sweet shop chain. The assets purchased are not being used to carry on the same kind of business and so there is no TOGC; Rupert must charge VAT on the sale of his shop.

It's vital that before a deal is done that the purchaser knows what the vendor has used the assets for prior to the sale and that the same type of business is carried on. The vendor must be satisfied that the purchaser has a genuine intention to carry on the same type of business. If the vendor is in any doubt, VAT must be charged.

9.3.3. Gap in trading

For the TOGC rules to apply there must be no significant gap in trading between the sale and purchase of the business. Where this occurs, the VATman can argue that there was no transfer of a going concern business.

TIP

There's no hard and fast time limit. For example, a reasonable break to allow for refurbishment, rebranding, etc. is OK.

9.4. THE NEED FOR REGISTRATION

If the vendor is VAT registered, there can only be a VAT-free TOGC if the purchaser is already registered at the date of transfer or becomes registered or liable to be registered as a result of the transfer.

> **TIP**
>
> Where you're purchasing a business and are not yet registered, it's sufficient, for the purposes of applying the TOGC rules, to have submitted an application to the VATman as an "intending trader". This is the case even where your registration hasn't been processed, as long as registration will apply (backdated if necessary) no later than the date the transfer of the business takes place.

Trap. When considering VAT registration in a TOGC situation, the vendor's turnover counts as if it were turnover of the purchaser. Thus, someone purchasing a VAT-registered business may become liable to VAT immediately as a result of the purchase.

9.4.1. Registration number

In a TOGC where you're the purchaser you can opt to take on the VAT registration number of the vendor, as long as they agree. This is usually to be avoided. The main benefit is being able to continue to use the same VAT registration number after the transfer.

> **TIP**
>
> Using the same registration number is helpful where, for example, you were in business as a sole trader or partnership and are now incorporating to a limited company. This will save you a great deal of time and trouble in the registration process.

Trap. Where you're buying a business from an unconnected vendor, taking on their VAT number means that you also take on any historic liabilities. So if a business is sold and the VAT number has been transferred, any errors on previous returns become your problem if further VAT is payable, or your benefit if a VAT refund is due. Our advice is that generally it's better to start a new registration.

Walter Walsingham sells his estate agency practice to Daisy Dunstable. She takes on his VAT registration number. At a subsequent VAT visit it comes to light that Walter never charged VAT on property management fees, only on sales commissions. He has under declared £75,000 of output tax. As Daisy has taken on the VAT registration number, she is liable.

EXAMPLE 2

Emily Ealing buys a Chinese restaurant from Ian Ipswich. She too takes on the VAT registration number. Having examined the previous returns she finds that Ian accounted for VAT on the gross takings each day even though this included tips. Emily knows that freely given tips are not consideration for any supply and so are outside the scope of VAT. She calculates that £42,000 of VAT has been accounted for on tips in this way in the last four years. She submits a claim which HMRC pays to her.

9.5.   BUYING PART OF A BUSINESS

The TOGC rules also recognise that it's possible to purchase part of a business and run it as a complete business in its own right.

EXAMPLE

Barry Birmingham's car dealership sells new and used cars and also has a workshop for servicing and repairs at the end of the yard. Barry decides that he wishes to concentrate on the dealing side only and sells the workshop, all of the tools, equipment and spare parts to Dermot Derry. There's no break in trading. Dermot has taken on sufficient assets to put him in a position to carry on the trade even though it wasn't the complete business he bought; it was a distinct separate business and so the TOGC rule applies and Barry doesn't need to charge VAT on the sale.

Note. There is a clear distinction; the part of the business sold as a TOGC must be capable of separate operation but there is no requirement that it's kept separate. If part of a business was capable of separate operation but in fact was incorporated into another business it would still be covered by the rules.

9.6.   SERIES OF SALES

Where there is a series of sales of a business, it's possible that the rules for relief will not be met, as the intermediary party may not carry on the trade. If this happens, VAT will be due.

EXAMPLE

George Glasgow wishes to retire and seeks to sell his design consultancy. One of his senior employees, Polly Paignton offers him £350,000 for the business, which he accepts. Contracts are drawn up and signed. A week later, before the deal is done, Lionel Leighton, a rival design consultant spots the advertisement in the trade press and contacts George with an offer of £385,000. George regretfully informs Lionel that he is too late as he has already agreed to sell to Polly. Lionel contacts Polly and offers her £385,000 and an extended contract with a £6,000 pay rise. Polly sees an immediate profit and accepts. A new contract, identical to the first, is drawn up between Polly and Lionel so she purchases and sells on the same day, simply taking her profit out of the middle. Polly has never carried on the business so there can be no TOGC relief, and so must add VAT to the sale price.

This highlights the need for the vendor (in this example George) to have a declaration of what the purchaser will use the assets for. If he did not know about the second sale, George could presume that the conditions were met and not charge VAT. The VATman would see the full picture and could seek to collect VAT from him.

As it's not a TOGC he needs to charge VAT. Polly will only be able to recover this tax by becoming VAT registered for a day!

9.6.1. Staged sales

Most businesses are sold all at once. However, it's possible to sell assets over a period of time with the intention of transferring a sufficient number to result in a business transfer. The fact that several sales may be made doesn't mean there can't be a TOGC, as long as the overall result is that of a business transfer.

9.7. INPUT TAX

As explained in previous chapters, VAT on purchases is recoverable only in so far as it relates to your business's taxable activity. The sale of a business as a going concern is outside the scope of VAT and doesn't meet this condition.

This means that VAT on sale costs is treated as residual input tax. Where the business being sold is fully taxable, full recovery is available, but if it's partially or fully exempt, the amount reclaimable will be restricted or not allowed at all.

9.8. SPECIAL RULES FOR LAND AND BUILDINGS

Where the assets being transferred consist partly or wholly of taxable buildings or land, there are some additional rules to take into consideration. In this context the phrase "taxable buildings and land" means land or buildings upon which VAT would be chargeable if the TOGC provisions did not apply. In practice, this means that either the vendor has made the option to apply VAT or the assets consist of the freehold of new commercial buildings (see Chapter 9).

9.8.1. Purchaser's option to tax land and buildings

For the sale to be a TOGC, the purchaser must opt to tax and notify HMRC of the option before the tax point for the transaction. The tax point is usually at completion rather than exchange of contracts.

Trap. Take care where a deposit is taken at the time contracts are exchanged. If a person, e.g. a conveyancing solicitor, takes a deposit as agent for the vendor rather than in the more usual, traditional stakeholder role, a VAT tax point occurs at this time. If the option to tax hasn't been made by then, it will mean that a taxable transaction has been made before the option and this will nullify the option.

Trap. Particular care also needs to be taken buying at auction where it's common for deposits to be payable by the successful bidder to the auctioneer who often acts as agent for the vendor. The VATman will normally accept a same-day notification of an option but to be on the safe side it's best to opt prior to attending the auction in respect of all potential bid targets. If unsuccessful in the bidding, the option can be easily revoked under the cooling-off period rules (see Chapter 9).

9.8.2. Anti-avoidance rules declaration

The purchaser must also make a declaration to the vendor that the option to tax anti-avoidance rules will not apply after the transfer (see Chapter 9). This declaration should also be made before the tax point.

These rules apply where the land or buildings are being sold as part of a large transfer and can also apply where the only assets being sold are the buildings and land.

EXAMPLE

The Chinese restaurant business sold by Ian Ipswich to Emily Ealing consisted of the building itself, the kitchen equipment and utensils, the furniture, other fixtures and fittings, the food and drink stocks and the use of the trading name. The building was opted to tax by Ian. If Emily also opts, the whole sale can be a TOGC and VAT-free. If she doesn't, the sale can still be a TOGC apart from the value ascribed to the building itself.

VAT will have to be charged on this. Emily will be able to recover this tax as input tax on her VAT return but will have to fund the VAT for a period of time.

She will also have a higher SDLT bill. SDLT is calculated on the amount paid, regardless of whether part of the amount paid is recoverable VAT. Having the purchase as a TOGC saves her money.

9.8.3. Selling a property on its own

Property rental is considered to be a business activity for VAT purposes. Thus, the sale of a let building (a property rental business) is sufficient to put the purchaser in possession of an asset of a business which can be continued. For example, a property investor who sells just one of their properties to someone else who intends to continue renting it out can treat the transfer as a TOGC.

The situations where a transfer of property counts as a TOGC are:

- a fully let building
- a partly let building where the rest is being advertised for letting
- an empty building where a tenant has signed a lease but not yet occupied the premises
- an empty building where a tenant is committed to entering into a lease albeit that the lease has not yet been signed.

There is no TOGC where there is:

- an empty building and no tenant in place or committed
- a let building but where the tenancy will end before completion, so that there is a vacant property at that time.

Trap. The sale of a property by a landlord to a tenant can't be a TOGC as the property will not be used for the same kind of business. The landlord has used it for a property rental business the tenant is to become an owner-occupier carrying on their own business.

Similarly, an immediate sub-sale of let property would not be a TOGC as the intermediary business will not carry on the business.

9.9. RECORDS

Where there is a TOGC, the vendor's records are still to be retained under the normal rules. There's no requirement for full records to pass to the purchaser unless the purchaser is taking on the vendor's VAT registration number.

If any of the assets being transferred are subject to the capital goods scheme (see Chapter 7), the purchaser takes on responsibility for any remaining VAT adjustment periods. The vendor must provide the purchaser with sufficient information to enable the calculations to be carried out, i.e.

- the original purchase price and VAT amount
- the original recovery percentage
- the number of adjustments remaining.

9.10. CHECKLIST

9.10.1. Vendor

If a vendor charges VAT incorrectly, there is little downside for them. The worst-case scenario is that there is a ruling that this was incorrect and the VAT should be repaid to the purchaser. This will result in a reduction in output tax with a corresponding credit from HMRC giving a neutral position. If VAT is not charged by mistake, the VATman can make an assessment for the lost VAT and may add a penalty. If the VAT can't be recovered from the purchaser, there is a significant and real cost.

Therefore, the vendor needs to have good quality documentary evidence before completing deals without VAT.

The vendor needs:

- proof that the purchaser is a taxable person, either registered already or liable to register as a result of the transfer
- a declaration of intention to carry on the same kind of business
- where taxable land and buildings are involved, proof of the option to tax by the purchaser; and
- the anti-avoidance rule declaration.

9.10.2. Purchaser

If a purchaser pays VAT incorrectly, it's not recoverable as input tax on a VAT return. The VATman could disallow the claim and leave the purchaser with a cost, which may not be recoverable from the vendor. The main benefits of TOGC treatment accrue to the purchaser, so the pressure to ensure compliance normally rests here.

The purchaser will want proof of:

- the vendor's VAT registration
- the use of the assets prior to the purchase
- the vendor's option to tax, where appropriate
- the age of the building, where appropriate.

9.11.   CONTRACT CLAUSES

As a vendor agreeing to TOGC treatment, you should include protective clauses in the sale/purchase contract to protect yourself against any comeback from the VATman. Whilst assuming that the TOGC treatment is correct, you'll wish to reserve the right to charge VAT should the VATman later rule that it was due. It's also a good idea to seek a guarantee that the purchaser will reimburse any interest and penalties charged by the VATman.

The purchaser might seek to protect themselves from later costs by stating that the transfer is believed to be covered by the TOGC provisions but if there is a subsequent ruling to the contrary, the purchase price is to be treated as VAT inclusive.

Clearly these positions are contradictory and only one can be put in the contract, so it's up to you to argue your case.

KEY POINTS

- the sale and purchase of a continuing business is outside the scope of VAT; this is known as a transfer of a going concern (TOGC)
- both the vendor and the purchaser must be VAT registered for the TOGC rules to apply
- the sale of part of a business that can be run by the purchaser in its own right counts as a TOGC
- selling a let commercial property counts as a TOGC providing the purchaser continues the business
- the TOGC rules won't apply where there's a gap between the vendor ceasing to run the business and the purchaser starting.

CHAPTER 10

Penalties

10.1. INTRODUCTION

There are three main situations where a business might incur penalties. It could be late in registering; late in submitting or paying its VAT returns, or it could make mistakes on those returns. Penalties cost UK businesses many millions of pounds each year. This is nearly always a cost that could be avoided.

10.2. WHAT IS "DEFAULT SURCHARGE"?

The default surcharge penalises businesses which are late in VAT return submission or payment. Each VAT return has a due date by which it has to be lodged with the VATman. If you miss this, he will impose a penalty known as a default surcharge.

The penalty varies according to compliance so the more often you're late, the higher the penalty can be.

10.2.1. First offence - warning letter

On the first occasion that a business is late paying or submitting a VAT return, the VATman issues a warning letter. This is called a "surcharge liability notice" (SLN); it's not a financial penalty, just a warning. It notifies the business that there has been a default, i.e. either the return or payment was late, and warns you that if it's late again within the following twelve months, a penalty will be levied.

If, for whatever reason, you're sent an SLN, you need to pull out all the stops to make sure that returns go in on time. If there's another late return within the SLN period, the VATman will either extend the period or charge you a financial penalty.

10.2.2. Penalty rate

If the business is late again in the SLN period (twelve months) a penalty is levied at the rate of 2% of the outstanding tax. This is the net tax shown as payable on the return less any payment that was made on time.

EXAMPLE

Alex Altrincham submits his VAT return for the March 2013 quarter late and receives an SLN. His November 2013 return is on time but he does not have sufficient funds to make payment. The return shows a net liability to HMRC of £40,000. A 2% penalty of £800 is levied.

Where you are unable to pay your VAT bill, you should pay as much as you can if you are in an SLN period. In our example above, had Alex made a part payment of, say, £10,000, the penalty would have been calculated on the reduced amount: £600.

10.2.3. What are the other consequences of being surcharged?

As well as being penalised, a new SLN period is notified, being twelve months from the previous default. A fully compliant business within this new SLN period will exit the penalty regime. However, if a further default occurs within this new twelve-month period, a further penalty will be imposed.

Second defaults are charged a 5% penalty; third penalties, 10%; fourth and subsequent penalties are at 15%.

All of the default surcharges are a minimum of £30, and, as a gesture to smaller businesses, the 2% and 5% penalties are not normally imposed where the amount of VAT involved is less than £400.

10.3. REASONS FOR A DELAY

10.3.1. Electronic submission problems

For most businesses postal delays aren't an issue as they are now required to submit their VAT returns online. However, it has been known for the VATman's online submission portal to appear to accept a return but not log it into the system, or for the portal website to be unavailable at times.

TIP

It's essential that you print all messages displayed on the submission system to back up any claims that a return was submitted or could not be submitted due to HMRC error. It's best to do this by making a screen print and pasting this into Word.

Download Zone

For a **Electronic Filing Checklist**, visit **http://books.indicator.co.uk**. You'll find the access code on page 2 of this book.

10.3.2. What counts as a reasonable excuse?

It's possible to argue against a penalty where you can show that there is a reasonable excuse for the lateness. To be successful it's usually required to prove that unforeseen circumstances beyond the business' control arose and gave rise to the default.

- **Insufficiency of funds.** Not having enough money to pay is specifically excluded from being a reasonable excuse. However, once again the courts and tribunals have stepped in to help businesses in this situation. Where your business has mostly been paid on time by its customers but has spent the money elsewhere instead of reserving it for the VAT payment, it wouldn't have a reasonable excuse. However, where you had every reason to expect to have the funds available but, for example, the sudden insolvency of a major customer means they can't pay you, in turn meaning you are unable to pay your VAT on time, the courts have agreed that this can be a reasonable excuse.

- **Reliance on a third party.** HMRC's view (and this is backed by the law) is that the business has a responsibility to submit its returns and payments on time. If it relies on someone else to do this for them, perhaps an accountant, that is a business decision but does not absolve them of responsibility if the return is late. But again, in extreme circumstances the courts have accepted that, for example, the sudden and critical illness of those responsible for preparing the VAT returns can be a reasonable excuse.

> ### TIP
>
> It's far better to avoid the penalty in the first place; have a back-up plan for preparing VAT returns in the event of a last-minute illness etc. of your bookkeeper. Make sure that the data to prepare the forms can be accessed in their absence. If both the normal and back-up arrangements fail, then you'll probably have a good chance of succeeding in an appeal against a penalty.

- **Ignorance of the law.** Not knowing your responsibilities or understanding the rules will not be accepted by the VATman as a reasonable excuse.

As a general rule, successful reasonable excuse claims tend to concern major disasters and sudden illnesses or even deaths. Lesser issues can constitute a reasonable excuse but usually only where several occur together.

Download Zone

For a **Reasonable Excuse Letter**, visit **http://books.indicator.co.uk**. You'll find the access code on page 2 of this book.

10.4. REGISTERING LATE

Late notification of liability to be registered is likely to result in a financial penalty. The level varies depending upon the reason for the lateness and how late the notification was made. Where the lateness was deliberate and the need to register was hidden from HMRC, the penalty is 100% of the tax which would have been due from the correct registration date to the date of notification. Where the lateness was deliberate but no steps were taken to hide this, the penalty is 70%. In all other cases the penalty is 30%, unless you can convince the VATman that you had acted reasonably at all times and that the delay was unavoidable.

TIP

Where you're aware that you've registered late, you can reduce the penalty by notifying the VATman before he finds out himself; this is called unprompted disclosure. Even where he finds out, you can still mitigate the penalty by coming clean with all the facts and figures; this is called prompted disclosure.

The penalties the VATman can charge are as follows:

MAXIMUM PENALTY	UNPROMPTED DISCLOSURE	PROMPTED
100%	30%	50%
70%	20%	35%
30%		
• less than twelve months late	Nil	10%
• twelve months late or more	10%	20%

10.5. ERRORS ON DOCUMENTS

Any error on a document that affects the amount of VAT payable can result in a penalty.

Trap. Penalties for errors on documents aren't just restricted to VAT returns. If a business tells the VATman about an error and makes mistakes in the figures again, this too can lead to a penalty. In fact, a penalty can be charged for any error in statement or correspondence that the VATman relies upon to establish the amount of VAT payable.

Trap. The penalty can also be imposed where the VATman gets things wrong!

EXAMPLE

Lucy London is suffering cash flow problems and decides to delay submission of her 04/11 VAT return. The VATman notices that the return has not been received and issues a central assessment, estimating that she owes £12,000. Lucy is delighted as she actually owes £21,000. She pays the assessment and then submits the return with the balancing payment two months later when she has received payment from her customer.

Lucy is liable to a penalty for not correcting the VATman's under-estimation.

TIP

Lucy could have avoided the penalty had she notified the VATman of the under-assessment within 30 days of the date of that assessment.

10.5.1. Rate of penalty

The rate of penalty varies depending upon the circumstances; in other words, what behaviour on the part of the business led to the mistake.

BEHAVIOUR	MAX PENALTY
Careless	30%
Deliberate but not concealed	70%
Deliberate and concealed	100%

TIP

The table above shows the maximum penalty that can be charged. These rates can be argued down, particularly if you act promptly and co-operatively to rectify the mistake, e.g. by paying the extra VAT due as soon as you become aware of an error.

10.5.2. The "reasonable care" get-out clause

The penalty provisions only apply where the business has either deliberately declared incorrect amounts or has done so by being careless. Therefore, if you take reasonable care to arrive at the correct result but make an innocent error, there can be no penalty. This throws the onus onto businesses to keep thorough records and where there's doubt over an action you take that has VAT consequences, you should keep detailed notes as to why you took the action you did.

EXAMPLE

Dan Dover introduces a new range of toasted sandwiches in his catering outlets. He is unsure whether the takeaway food will constitute standard-rated catering or zero-rated cold takeaway food. He reads through a variety of sources and finds that there is some area for doubt in interpretation, as some businesses have won tribunal appeals on this subject whereas others have failed. He takes a balanced approach and decides that his particular products more closely resemble the zero-rated items in the successful appeals. He accounts for no VAT on these sales. Two years later the VATman visits and takes the opposite view and raises an assessment to recover the VAT undeclared. A penalty is also imposed. Dan argues that he was not acting carelessly and produces his notes of his research and thought process. Whilst accepting their decision that the tax is due, no penalty should be charged.

10.5.3. Deliberate but not concealed errors

Why would anyone deliberately understate a VAT liability and not try to hide the fact? This might seem like odd behaviour but there can be times when this approach makes sense. It might be that the VATman and the business disagree over the correct treatment of certain supplies. The business may decide to maintain their treatment pending resolution of the discussion. They are deliberately declaring an amount of tax that is incorrect under the VATman's interpretation but are not hiding the fact.

10.5.4. Mitigating penalties

The penalties can be reduced through disclosure of information and co-operation. If an error is found by the business and reported to HMRC (an unprompted disclosure) greater mitigation is available than if HMRC asks questions first and data is disclosed as a result of this (prompted disclosure).

The minimum penalties following mitigation for disclosure are:

BEHAVIOUR	UNPROMPTED DISCLOSURE	PROMPTED DISCLOSURE
Careless	0%	15%
Deliberate not concealed	20%	35%
Deliberate and concealed	30%	50%

Note. The percentages given in the table are a minimum. Owning up to an error does not automatically qualify for full mitigation. This will only be considered where, as a starting point, full detail is given of:

• the nature of the errors
• how and why they arose
• the amounts involved, broken down into VAT periods.

10.5.5. Suspended penalties

The VATman can suspend penalties resulting from careless behaviour (not deliberate errors), for example by not having a proper system of record keeping which has resulted in the incorrect figures on VAT returns. This means that the business doesn't have to pay the penalty but instead has to comply with whatever reasonable conditions the VATman wants to impose.

These conditions will be put in writing and will usually involve the implementation of new systems or processes to ensure that future errors are avoided. If the business complies with the requirements for a specified period of time (usually two years), the penalty will be cancelled. If the requirements are not met, the penalty will be enforced.

> **TIP**
>
> Where you've made an error in one or more VAT returns because of a failure in your accounting systems, it's worth volunteering to the VATman to improve them and asking whether the penalty can be suspended.

10.5.6. Appealing against a penalty

If the VATman imposes a penalty, the business can appeal to the tribunal against the categorisation of the error, i.e. the rate at which it's levied or the level of mitigation given.

If the error is classed as being careless, and the VATman doesn't allow suspension or imposes overly onerous conditions, these too are decisions that can be appealed against. Appendix 4 gives information on how to appeal.

Download Zone

For an **Internal Review Letter** and an **Authority Letter to the Taxman**, visit **http:// books.indicator.co.uk**. You'll find the access code on page 2 of this book.

- the VATman can impose penalties for: paying VAT late, submitting VAT returns late, registering later than required, and making errors on VAT returns or other documents
- the penalty for late payments and returns is called a surcharge and starts at 2% of the VAT declared or paid late but can be up to 15%
- the VATman will cancel a surcharge if you can prove to him you had a reasonable excuse for the lateness
- penalties for late registration range from 30% to 100% of the VAT lost or declared late as a result
- penalties for errors on documents range from 30% to 100% of the VAT lost
- all penalties, but not surcharges, can be reduced by negotiation with the VATman
- where you acted reasonably but made an innocent error, the VATman can't charge a penalty.

CHAPTER 11

Schemes for promoting your business

11.1. INTRODUCTION

Business promotion schemes vary immensely in their structure and operation but all have the aim of increasing market presence, turnover and customer base. One common theme is that they usually entail creating an environment in which someone obtains goods or services either free of charge or at a reduced rate. This can pose a problem in deciding what supplies are being made or what their value is for the purpose of calculating VAT output tax. The schemes can also affect the amount of input VAT a business can reclaim.

11.2. BUSINESS GIFTS

Some promotion schemes involve simply giving away goods free of charge.

Trap. Something given in exchange for something else isn't a gift, even if no money changes hands. It counts as a supply where the consideration, i.e. the amount treated as paid, is the market value of the goods.

A gift of goods counts as a supply for VAT purposes. This means that you can reclaim VAT on the cost of the item you give away. It also means than output tax is due on the gift unless the cost of such gifts to any one person is no more than £50 per annum, in which case the output tax is waived. Any VAT is calculated on the cost to the business of giving the gift, i.e. for a gift that was purchased for this purpose, its cost, whether the goods were manufactured in-house, and the cost of production.

Note. A case recently heard in the European Court (EMI Group Plc) ruled that gifts made to different people within the same organisation each have a £50 limit. So, for example, if you're making a Christmas gift to five employees that work for one of your corporate customers and the gifts are worth £40 each, you don't have to account for VAT on these even though the total value is £200.

> TIP
>
> Only gifts of goods that would normally bear VAT if you sold them will attract a VAT charge. So consider making gifts of zero-rated goods, e.g. most food items, as these don't give rise to a tax charge.

> TIP
>
> A gift of services will normally be VAT-free, e.g. a free beauty or health treatment, as they usually only occur where there is payment. But these can include a hidden gift of goods.

Trap. Where the service given away is free use of goods, a supply does occur and is to be valued using the cost to the business of providing it, e.g. a free beauty treatment is likely to include use of some products, oils etc. VAT on the cost of the products used would have to be accounted for.

11.2.1.   Discount schemes

Genuine reductions in price to attract more custom are a common way of promoting business. The scale of such discounts is immaterial as long as you're not connected to the person or organisation you're offering the discount to. VAT is only chargeable on the discounted price.

Discounts can be offered in advance or given as a reward, perhaps for achieving a certain volume of purchases. The effect is the same for VAT purposes.

EXAMPLE

Immie Trading sells bicycles on a wholesale basis to cycle shops in the UK. It offers a 10% discount to shops that purchase more than 60 each year. It sells bicycles to Rupert Ripon for sale through his shop at £250 each. Rupert typically purchases eight bicycles each month and so he exceeds the 60 limit in August each year. Immie Trading invoices for the full value until that date as the promotion limit has not been reached. A credit note is issued in August to reflect the previous purchases and Immie Trading can adjust its next return to account for this reduction in VAT.

11.2.2.   Buy one get one free etc.

This is a misnomer as far as the VATman is concerned. In reality, you're not selling one item at full price and offering the other one as a gift. If this were the case VAT would be due on the full price of the gift unless it's covered by the £50 rule mentioned above. In practice, you should look at it as selling two items each at 50%.

The same applies to other variations on the same theme, e.g. "buy three for the price of two", and schemes where a different product is given alongside the goods being promoted.

EXAMPLE

Douglas is seeking to increase sales of printing paper. He offers a free memory stick with each order of ten or more reams. The memory stick is not really "free", it's paid for through the purchase price of the paper.

11.2.3. Difference in VAT rates on gifted goods

Where the "free goods" you're offering as an incentive are subject to the same rate of VAT as the goods that are being given away, you can apply the VAT to the sale price without having to make any adjustment. But where a different VAT rate applies to the reward goods, you can apportion the income received between the chargeable item and the free item which can save you VAT.

EXAMPLE

Donald Dundee has written a history of the telescope. He offers purchasers of telescopes a free copy of the printed book. These books are not really free but part of the overall deal. Donald can attribute a portion of the total sales price to the book, which is zero-rated and so save himself some tax. In other words, he can say that as the price of the book to those who don't buy his telescopes is £10.00 including (VAT is at 0% on printed books) he can knock this off the price he received for the telescope. If he charges £100 including VAT of £20 for the telescope sold on its own, he would have to pay £20 over to the VATman. But where he throws in the zero-rated book worth £10 he only has to account for VAT on £90, i.e. £18.

11.2.4. Linked supply concession

Linked supplies of this nature are covered by a concession from HMRC which can be adopted if appropriate. This is often useful in the publishing industry. Many publishers produce magazines with cover-mounted items which often have a different VAT liability to the magazine which is zero-rated.

TIP

Where a cover-mounted item represents less than 20% of the total price, and this is less than £1 if it's a normal retail item or £5 for a non-retail item, the VAT rate of the main product can be used for the cover-mounted item as well. This avoids the need to apportion values between them.

TIP

This rule is only a concession and so doesn't have to be followed. Where the linked item is zero-rated and the main one standard-rated, using the apportionment method will produce a better result.

Schemes for promoting your business

11

11.2.5. More than one business

Where the business devising and promoting the scheme is separate from the business providing the promotional goods, things can get a little more complicated.

EXAMPLE 1

Andrew St Andrews has invented a new type of golf ball. He decides that it would be a good idea to have as many people as possible try it out. He approaches a golf magazine and offers it 10,000 free balls to put on the cover of the next issue.

As the value of the balls is more than £50, he has an output tax liability calculated on the cost to him of providing them. The magazine has no output tax liability due to the operation of the linked goods concession.

TIP

If Andrew agreed to provide the balls in return for a full-page advertisement in the magazine, then the value to be used for output tax purposes could be the value of the advertisement rather than the cost of the balls.

TIP

An alternative way to dodge this VAT problem would be to get the publisher to give the balls to the individuals buying the magazine as his agent. They would have to make it clear to the magazine buyer that it was the golf ball manufacturer that was giving away the free ball. If they do this, each gift would fall below the £50 limit, so there would be no output tax for the manufacturer or the magazine to account for.

11.3. TIMING OF VAT ON DISCOUNTS

The different methods of offering discounts as described above can result in getting the VAT benefit at different times, and this should be taken into account when deciding which scheme to use.

EXAMPLE

Sheila Sheffield makes shampoo. To promote a new range she wants to use a "three for two" offer. However, as she sells through retailers it will be they who have to promote the offer in store.

Sheila could sell:

- the shampoo to the retailers at a discount on the condition that they operated the promotion. In this case she would only have an output tax liability on the discounted price

- at normal prices and then issue a credit note to reimburse the retailers on their costs. This would mean full output tax at the outset with a reduction when the credit note was issued

- at normal prices and pay the retailers a fee for operating the scheme. In this case she would have to account for VAT output tax on the sale price and reclaim input VAT on the fee from the retailer.

11.4. MONEY-OFF COUPONS

Money-off coupons entitle the bearer to a discount on the purchase of specified items. They could be distributed on their own or perhaps form part of the packaging on goods.

EXAMPLE

Sheila Sheffield also manufactures toothpaste. On the packaging of a particular brand which is underperforming she decides to include a "25p off next purchase" coupon. The normal price for the toothpaste is £2.75.

When the customer purchases the first tube, £2.75 is paid and the retailer accounts for VAT accordingly. When the coupon is redeemed, the next tube is sold for only £2.50. VAT is due on the £2.50 received by the retailer. At this stage the retailer has made less profit than usual through the operation of the promotion scheme. Sheila gives the retailer a contribution of 20p per unit to compensate them.

Again, this can be done through the issue of a credit note against the original goods sale or treated as a supply by the retailer operating the scheme.

11.5. CASH-BACK SCHEMES

Cash-back schemes are similar to money-off schemes, the difference being that the member of the public pays the full amount and is then given money back rather than paying a discounted amount.

The main difference is that it's usually the manufacturer rather than the retailer who makes good the cash-back payment.

EXAMPLE

Barry Birmingham has a car dealership. A manufacturer offers a £2,000 cash-back on one of their models normally costing £25,000. The purchaser pays the full retail price to Barry who accounts for VAT accordingly.

The manufacturer pays £2,000 to the individual under the cash-back promotion. The overall effect of this is that the individual has really bought a car for £23,000 not £25,000 but VAT has been accounted for on £25,000. The manufacturer can reduce its output tax liability to reflect this.

11.6. FACE VALUE VOUCHERS

Face value vouchers (FVV) are coupons which have a cash equivalent value printed upon them and which can be used for payment or part payment for goods and/or services. A common example of this would be a gift token. As a general rule they are treated as being equivalent to cash.

TIP

FVVs are a good way to make sales without immediately having to account for VAT, as there's no VAT on the sale of these as long as it's at face value or less. But where, for example, a £10 token is sold for £10.25 to reflect the cost of the greetings card which is provided, VAT is due on 25p.

Note. Only when the voucher is redeemed is the value treated as payment for the goods or services and so VAT triggered.

EXAMPLE

Rupert Ripon's bicycle shop sells a £20 token to Jenny Jarrow. There's no VAT on this sale. Jenny gives the voucher to her son Johnny for his birthday and he uses it as part payment against a new cycle helmet costing £35, paying cash for the balance of £15. Rupert treats this as a sale for £35 and accounts for VAT accordingly. As cycle helmets are zero-rated there is no tax charge. Had Johnny used the token to pay for new lights for his bicycle, VAT would have been due at the standard rate.

If an FVV is given away instead of being sold, there's no VAT consequence to the gift of the voucher but there could be an issue on redemption. The goods or services would be provided against a freely given voucher, meaning that there was no consideration for the supply. The business gifts rule would therefore apply when the FVV is redeemed.

11.7. LOYALTY AND STORE CARDS

Store loyalty cards offer incentives to individuals to shop at particular outlets, usually by awarding points which can be redeemed as part or full payment for future purchases of goods or services.

Schemes that award cash value to the cardholder for purchases are effectively giving a discount on future purchases. The use of the card requires full payment for the goods being purchased initially, the discount being available only against future transactions. When the points etc. are redeemed against goods or services, VAT is only chargeable on the reduced price.

Points schemes can work in one of three ways:

1. The points can convert into face value vouchers. If this is the case, the VAT treatment of the vouchers is the same as a discount voucher, see above.

2. The points could be redeemed against goods or services which have an equivalent points value. In this case the goods are viewed as gifts.

> **TIP**
>
> As the points system doesn't allocate a face value to a voucher it can't be considered to be payment, and so when the points are exchanged for goods this is a gift and VAT doesn't have to be accounted for unless it exceeds the £50 limit over one year.

3. The points could be redeemed by third parties, e.g. a Nectar card. In this case the redemption gives rise to an output tax charge by the third party, either under the gift rules if there is no payment, or under the discount rules where the customer has to pay something for the reward goods; where the operator of the points promotion scheme pays the retailer, the normal VAT rules apply. In this case the promoter of the scheme will be eligible to reclaim this VAT as input tax as a cost of its business.

11.8.   LOTTERY SCHEMES

Some schemes operate by giving a lottery ticket, e.g. a scratch card, to purchasers of goods or services. The supply of the card itself doesn't trigger VAT.

* if a winning card gives entitlement to a discount, then the normal discount rules apply

* if a winning card awards free goods or services, the gift rules apply

* if the winner receives a cash payment, there is no VAT.

11.9.   DEALER LOADER SCHEMES

These schemes are similar to retrospective volume discounts. A dealer loader scheme is where a business gives free items once a certain level of purchases is achieved.

Where the reward goods are to be used in the purchaser's business, the VATman sees the original sales price as also covering the reward goods. And where the goods will be used for private purposes, the VATman sees the reward goods as gifts.

11.10. LOW VALUE TRADE-IN SCHEMES

A true low value trade-in scheme offers a product at a discount on the condition that a specified item is given in return.

EXAMPLE

Sarah Salford sells paint. She runs a promotion whereby a customer can get £2 off a tin of paint if they bring in any old paint tin. As long as there is some paint in the old tin, Sarah will award the discount.

If a tin of paint normally sells for £20 she will only charge £18 with the trade in. Clearly, there is no real value in the trade in item and Sarah only accounts for VAT on the £18 received; the value of the old tin is not deemed to be the £2 difference and consideration for the supply.

This must not be confused with the true part-exchange where a customer can negotiate a value for an item being offered in part-exchange. There, the full value of the goods being sold must be used for calculating output tax.

KEY POINTS

- VAT is not payable on the value of business gifts you make which have a value of £50 or less
- gifts to the same person or organisation worth more than £50 over the course of the year are subject to VAT
- gifts attached to another product, e.g. a CD with a magazine, usually follow the VAT treatment of the main goods being sold
- where you give a discount on goods or services, VAT is only accountable on the discounted price
- points or value awarded in a loyalty scheme, store card etc. are ignored for VAT purposes until they are redeemed for a free or reduced price item. VAT then only applies to the discounted value of the goods.

Schemes for promoting your business

CHAPTER 12

VAT and your business premises

12.1. INTRODUCTION

The VAT rules which apply to property are long-winded. And those relating to the construction, buying, selling, leasing and renting are particularly involved so we've included an appendix to explain them. In this chapter we consider only the day-to-day transactions you might make in connection with your business premises.

12.2. VAT ON REPAIRS AND MAINTENANCE

For VAT purposes, the purchase of materials and services to repair or improve your business premises are treated like any other that you make. This means that you can reclaim the VAT paid.

The only exceptions to this rule are where:

- the construction cost £250,000 or more - in this case the capital goods scheme applies
- your business is partly exempt - in this case the partial exemption rules apply.

12.2.1. Employing a builder

Where you've employed a builder to carry out the repairs or improvements, find out whether they're VAT registered before they start work. If you're using a one-man-band to just decorate, you may find they're not VAT registered, whereas a building firm which employs workers almost certainly will be. This can play a part in deciding how to purchase the materials for the job.

TIP

Where you're using an unregistered worker to do some work and this involves materials, e.g. paint, plaster etc., either purchase the materials yourself or give the builder the cash to buy it on your behalf, and make sure the receipt/invoice is in your business' name. In this way you can reclaim the VAT on the materials, whereas if the builder bought and supplied them, you would not. And if you decide to do the job yourself, you can still reclaim the VAT paid on the cost of materials.

12.3.   HOME OFFICE

12.3.1.   Does a home office count as a business premises?

Whether your business is run from an office suite, factory or shop, you might also have an office set up at home for when you need to work out of normal hours. You may even run your company entirely from your private residence. The good news is that the VATman doesn't discriminate against costs you incur in improving or repairing your home office. As long as you are spending the money for business purposes, you can reclaim the VAT you pay. But again, make sure the invoices are in the business' name and paid for or reimbursed by it.

12.3.2.   Creating an office or workshop at home

Where you want to create a workspace at home you have two main alternatives: convert an existing room, loft or garage, or build a new structure, say, in the garden. As the cost is incurred for a business purpose, you can reclaim the VAT on both the materials and labour.

TIP

The latter idea has become so popular that there are companies which produce ready-made office/workshop modules for your garden; worth a look if you don't fancy the DIY approach or turning your home into a building site.

Trap. Where you expect to use the work area for non-business purposes, you can't reclaim all the VAT and an adjustment has to be made (see below).

EXAMPLE

Mike Margate is the MD of a manufacturing company. His role is mainly clerical and he wants to carry out more of it at home. He decides to construct an office in his garden and will get his company to pay for it. It will cost £10,000 plus £2,000 VAT for the work to be carried out by a builder. Mike estimates he will use the office for personal work for about 20% of the time. His company is entitled to claim 80% of the input VAT.

12.3.3.   What happens when the house is sold?

EXAMPLE CONTINUED

After five years Mike sells his house to someone who intends to use it just as their private residence. Mike's company is not allowed to charge VAT on the sale of the office because it's going to be used as part of the dwelling, and so

---

is exempt. As it was built on Mike's land as a permanent structure, it probably has no rights to any of the sale proceeds, but that's a legal issue not a VAT one. The main VAT point is that the company is not required to repay any of the VAT it reclaimed at the time of purchase.

TIP

If VAT is to be claimed by a company, the invoices for the building work, etc. must be issued in the company's name, not that of the director.

12.3.4. Converting part of your home

The same principle applies to the VAT you pay on the cost of converting part of your home for work use. Whether you're a limited company paying for work at an employee's or director's home, or a sole trader or member of a partnership, you can reclaim VAT on the costs of converting part of your home to business use. Again, the invoices etc. for the work should be in the name of the business, but in the case of a partner or sole trader this is not vital, just preferable.

When it comes to selling your home which includes the converted office space, this will be VAT exempt, and no claw back of the VAT is made, even if you sell the property just a year after conversion.

12.3.5. Home office equipment

The apportionment of VAT on the equipment used in your home/workshop doesn't have to be restricted in the same way that it does on the construction costs. So, for example, the VAT on the cost of a computer which is used 100% for business can be reclaimed in full, even where the office is used only, say, 80% of the time for work.

Trap. Where the office is used for non-business reasons, the VAT on the cost of desks, chairs etc. is likely to need apportioning in the same percentage as the cost of construction.

TIP

Don't forget the VAT paid on your home office/workshop lighting and heating costs. The VAT rules say that you can claim a fair and reasonable proportion of this too. But it must be the business and not the householder who is liable for the bill. Sole traders have an advantage over companies and partnerships here as bills in their own name will be OK. Companies and partnerships should arrange for the energy contract to be in their name.

12.4. SELLING OFFICE EQUIPMENT

Where you sell office furniture and fittings, you must charge VAT at the standard rate, except where you didn't reclaim the VAT on the purchase because none was charged; typically, this might be where you purchased it second-hand.

TIP

Where you give assets to your employees, say, an old office desk, you don't have to charge output VAT or repay any of the input VAT you claimed on the purchase.

Note. "Give" means that you received nothing from the employee in exchange.

KEY POINTS

- VAT paid on the costs of repairing and improving your business premises can be reclaimed
- your business can reclaim the VAT on adding to or converting part of your home to business use
- where you intend to use your home office or workshop for non-business purposes, you can only reclaim input VAT in proportion to your expected business use
- selling a home which includes an office/workshop is exempt and will not trigger a claw back of VAT reclaimed.

CHAPTER 13

International trade

13.1. INTRODUCTION

Trading internationally brings its own challenges and rewards. As a general rule, where goods leave the UK they will be zero-rated, but there are some exceptions, notably supplies to private individuals in other EU states. Failure to comply with the record keeping requirements usually means you'll have to account for VAT on the transaction in question.

Goods entering the UK give rise to a VAT charge as if they were being supplied here. Businesses can usually recover this VAT as if it were input tax, but failure to follow the many rules correctly could prove costly as you can lose the right to reclaim VAT.

Supplying or receiving services, as opposed to goods, cross border is rather more complex and there are some very detailed rules for determining when and in which country VAT becomes due. Get it wrong and, again, you could be picking up the VAT bill.

13.2. EXPORTS - GENERAL RULES

The word "export" is given a particular meaning in VAT terminology. It relates to the movement of goods out of the UK for a destination outside of the EU. If the goods are destined for another member state of the EU, they would be referred to as despatches or distance sales and the treatment would be different (see below).

Under basic VAT rules, goods which are physically located in the UK at the commencement of their journey are treated as supplied here and so are subject to UK VAT. However, under an international agreement, the world's trading community operates under what's known as a destination system. The effect of the destination system is to levy VAT where the goods end their journey rather than under the normal place of supply rules. Consequently, exported goods are specifically relieved of UK VAT, making them zero-rated.

As with all of the zero-rating provisions, this only applies where certain criteria are met. These relate to the status of the customer, the timing of the movement and the documentation held as evidence of the export.

TIP

You can reclaim VAT on the cost of all goods you export even where you don't have to charge VAT to your customer.

13.3. WHEN CAN YOU ZERO-RATE A SUPPLY OF GOODS?

The export can only be zero-rated when the goods are supplied to a qualifying person. These are defined as:

- a person not resident in the UK
- a trader who has no business establishment in the UK from which taxable supplies are made
- an overseas authority.

Additionally, you are not allowed to zero-rate goods where the customer is UK VAT registered.

13.4. ZERO-RATING TIME LIMITS

To qualify for zero-rating, the goods must physically leave the UK for a place outside the EU within certain time limits.

Trap. Failure to meet the time limit will mean VAT is due at the rate applicable had the goods been supplied in the UK. If you've already agreed a price with your customer, you may have to account for the VAT without the prospect of getting it back.

For supplies of goods where the supplier is responsible for the movement, the time limit is three months. The same limit applies where the goods are delivered in the UK to an export agent consolidator for onward delivery outside the UK.

A further three months is allowed if delivery is made in the UK to someone who will carry out a process on the goods prior to delivery outside the EU.

Trap. It's not sufficient that the goods are exported within the time frame, you'll also have to prove it with documentary evidence. The evidence should be obtained within the same time limit noted above and retained as inspectors will look closely at exports.

SAD form. All goods travelling internationally outside the EU or moving in or out of it should be declared using a Single Administrative Document (Form C88). The UK supplier of export goods should have a copy of this form for each export shipment for which zero-rating is claimed.

Other commercial documentation. There's no definitive list of documents that are required to prove export has taken place but these may include bills of lading and air waybills, certificates of shipment and proofs of posting.

13.4.1. Customer status

If any doubt exists as to the status of the customer, then a declaration should be obtained from them that they qualify for zero-rating. Where you are responsible for exporting the goods and so have control over the timing and documentation, little difficulty should be encountered. However, if the goods are to be delivered in the UK to a shipper or processor or directly to the customer in an ex-works transaction, there is less certainty. Control of the movement has passed to someone else meaning that delays could occur which can't be foreseen or perhaps even known about. Documentation will not necessarily pass automatically to everyone who needs it.

TIP

If there's doubt over whether zero-rating can apply, it's a sensible precaution to agree with your customer that they pay an amount equal to the VAT that would be due if the goods weren't exported. The payment can be returned in full once the goods have gone and the documentation to back this up has been received.

13.5. IMPORTS

The word "import" also has a special meaning in VAT and refers to the supply of goods which involves their removal from a place outside the UK and their entry into the UK.

There are a variety of methods for declaring goods to Customs. The basic and simplest is still the completion of the SAD form and its presentation to Customs at the time of importation. However, the information can be provided in advance (pre-entry) or in summary form with full declarations being submitted later (period entry). Most agents use electronic versions of these forms and transmit the information directly to Customs.

13.6. VALUING OF IMPORTS

The main requirement for the release of imported goods is the payment of indirect taxes. First, any duty is calculated and then any VAT.

VAT is generally calculated using a CIF (cost, insurance and freight) valuation plus any Customs Duty, and is charged at the rate appropriate for the goods, e.g. books which are normally zero-rated in the UK will not be subject to import VAT, but television sets will be.

13.6.1. Cost

Cost will most commonly be the transaction where goods have been purchased. Alternative costing methods are available for goods in other circumstances.

For VAT purposes, insurance and freight are declared to the point of first delivery in the UK. This means that for goods arriving at, say, Heathrow Airport and being offloaded on to a lorry and driven straight to a customer's premises in Surrey, the insurance and freight cost is that to Surrey, not only to Heathrow or to UK airspace as could be the case with duty.

EXAMPLE

Goods costing £6,000 have been imported through Heathrow and delivered by lorry to Surrey. The insurance and freight costs to Surrey were £1,000. There was a duty rate of 2.5% on the goods and this was calculated to be £168.75 (remember, the value for duty and VAT can differ).

	£
Goods	6,000.00
Insurance and freight	1,000.00
Duty	168.75
Total	7,168.75
VAT at 20%	1,433.75

13.6.2. Payment

The basic principle is that any duty and VAT become due at the point of entry and the goods are not released until the taxes have been paid. This can be done at the time of importation.

TIP

Instead of paying VAT on import you can use HMRC's duty and VAT deferment scheme. As the name suggests, this allows the duty and VAT to be paid later. This is good for cash flow and can also have the effect of speeding up the clearance process. The advantages of this are clear but are counterbalanced slightly by some disadvantages. Firstly, the need to become authorised. However, the application process is fairly simple, consisting of the completion of three forms:

- C1200 - the application form itself. Not too complex, merely giving some details of the applicant

- C1201 - guarantee form. Customs will not approve anyone unless a suitable guarantee is provided. This is usually in the form of a bank guarantee
- the guarantee will be to a set limit. No account can be left open as to value. You decide what the appropriate level will be, bearing in mind the amount of VAT and/or duty you wish to defer.

> **TIP**
>
> If you have a seasonal trade, the limit can be set to vary from season to season if preferred.

Under certain circumstances Customs will now allow duty and VAT deferment without a guarantee. Applications will be approved where Customs feel that there is a good compliance record and low risk.

- C1202 - direct debit mandate. The payment is collected on the 15th of the month following the importation using direct debit
- a further form - C1207 - will be required if you are to use an agent to clear goods on your behalf and wish them to use your deferment account.

> **TIP**
>
> If the value of the tax which you wish to defer exceeds the limit, you could seek to increase the limit, though this is resisted by HMRC if you wish to then reduce it soon after. It prefers limits to remain fairly constant unless there's an obvious trend either up or down.

If you don't wish to increase the limit, you can either pay the excess at the port or airport or perhaps use another business's account. The deferment system is simply a payment mechanism and so Customs are not too bothered who pays as long as someone does. Import agents will normally have their own accounts which they will clear goods through on your behalf.

13.6.3. Reclaiming import VAT

The VAT incurred on the importation of goods is recoverable on VAT returns in the same way as VAT incurred on the purchase of goods in the UK.

The requirements are therefore similar. The goods must have been imported by a business for the purposes of that business in the course of making taxable supplies. And, of course, you have to be able to prove it and have the appropriate evidence.

In the case of UK purchases it's usually necessary to have a tax invoice to evidence the VAT input tax claim. Where goods are imported, the supplier of the goods has not charged tax, rather Customs has. It's therefore Customs who provides the documentation.

This comes in the form of Certificate C79 which comes once a month, generated on or around the 11th of the month following the importation. It's addressed to the person declared as the importer on the entry declaration, C88. Thus, whether the goods are imported through your own duty deferment account or someone else's, the C79 is still in your name and this is the document for input tax recovery.

If the tax has been paid through an agent's deferment account, an invoice will be rendered to recover the VAT. This invoice should not be used for input tax recovery but reliance placed on the C79.

The tax incurred and shown on the C79 is recoverable on the VAT return covering the period of importation. Thus, a C79 dated July 11 will reflect imports in June and the tax can be claimed on the return covering June.

Where you wish to import goods and recover the input VAT but aren't yet registered, there would be no C79 against which to recover tax. To get around this problem, Customs will issue you with a temporary number which can be used for the purpose of C79.

13.7. EU SUPPLIES DESPATCHES

As with exports, despatches are UK supplies but specifically relieved of UK VAT through zero-rating. As long as the criteria are met, the supply is relieved of VAT but if any conditions are not met, UK VAT applies.

13.7.1. What's a despatch?

A despatch is simply the movement of goods from one member state of the EC to another, where the person receiving the goods in the member state of destination is VAT registered in a different member state than the person from whom the goods are moving. This could include movements of own goods from one state to another without change of ownership. There doesn't have to be a sale for there to be a despatch.

The zero-rating conditions are:

1. The goods must physically leave the UK and enter another member state. The mode of transport is immaterial as long as the goods have moved.

2. The movement must take place within certain time limits.

    (a) If the goods are moved directly to their destination in the other member state or are delivered in the UK to a shipper or forwarder for consolidation, the goods must leave the UK within three months of the transaction, (usually date of invoice).

    (b) Where goods are delivered in the UK to another business which will carry out some sort of process work on them prior to despatch, the time limit extends to six months.

3. Proof must be held of the movement and its timing. Documentary evidence that the goods have gone must be held. The more paperwork that can be obtained the better. Great care must be taken over this, especially where control over the movement passes to someone else, e.g. ex-works sales.

    The VATman states that proof of dispatch documents must show:

    *   date of departure of goods from the supplier
    *   customer's name, VAT number, a description of the goods and an invoice number
    *   registration number of the vehicle collecting the goods and the name and signature of the driver
    *   delivery address for the goods
    *   name and address for consolidation, groupage, or processing (if applicable)
    *   route (e.g .Channel Tunnel, port of exit)
    *   name of ferry or shipping company and date of sailing (if applicable); and
    *   airway bill number and airport (if applicable).

    The information held should also include the following:

    *   trailer number (if applicable)
    *   full container number (if applicable); and
    *   name and address of the haulier collecting the goods.

    The VATman suggests that you can get this information from:

    *   commercial transport document(s) from the carrier responsible for removing the goods from the UK
    *   customer's order
    *   inter-company correspondence
    *   copy sales invoice
    *   advice note
    *   packing list
    *   details of insurance or freight charges
    *   evidence of payment
    *   evidence of receipt of goods abroad; and
    *   any other documents relevant to the removal of the goods in question which you would normally obtain in the course of your intra-EU business.

4. The customer must be VAT registered in another member state of the EU.

Trap. If the customer can't provide a valid VAT registration number from another state, then the supply is treated as a UK supply and UK VAT is due.

It should be noted that the requirement is not that the customer is registered in the same member state into which the goods are being moved but in one of the other states. Thus, a French customer could use a French VAT number to obtain VAT-free goods being sent to Italy.

It's prudent to check that the VAT number being quoted is valid. There is a significant amount of VAT fraud in the EU involving the use of bogus or stolen VAT numbers to obtain VAT-free goods.

Trap. Strictly, if a VAT number quoted is invalid the zero-rating does not apply and so there could be a real tax cost to the supplier.

All numbers should be checked. As a minimum you should ensure that they conform with the relevant format for the country. Each state has a unique format for its VAT registration numbers and this should be considered. Secondly, it's recommended that all VAT numbers from new customers are checked with the VIES system available at http://ec.europa.eu/taxation_customs/vies

5. The customer's VAT registration number must be shown on the sales invoice along with the two-character country identifier.

13.8. DISTANCE SALES

Distance selling is the term used to describe sales of goods to persons in other member states but where the customer has not given a valid VAT number which is needed for zero-rating.

Where a VAT registration number isn't supplied, zero-rating won't apply and so the supply must be treated as if it were an ordinary UK supply and the appropriate rate of VAT applied accordingly.

This is the basic rule and applies unless and until the distance selling thresholds are reached. These are limits which have been introduced by each member state to avoid tax loss through cross border shopping. For example, some books when sold within Denmark attract the full 25% standard rate of VAT. When sold in the UK these same books would be zero-rated. If they could be sold by mail order or over the Internet from the UK to Danish customers, there would be an obvious advantage.

Trap. The thresholds can require registration for VAT in the customers' country under certain circumstances, and so if you make a lot of distance sales in one particular EU state you'll need to keep an eye on the registration threshold for that country (see Appendix 5).

Unless registration in the other country is necessary, you should treat EU sales as if they were ordinary UK ones. Once registered in the other country you'll be given a VAT number there. This will then mean sales can be zero-rated; the requirement to show the registration number of your customer is achieved by showing your registration number in the foreign state. Of course, as you'll be registered for VAT in the other state, you'll have to account for the VAT there.

EXAMPLE

Lexie Lewis is a book dealer. She sells books to the Danish public. She zero-rates her sales supplies until she reaches the Danish distance sales threshold of Euro 37,551. Having reached this limit she must register for Danish VAT and charge local rate VAT of 25%.

13.9. INTERNATIONAL SERVICES

The rules for determining whether VAT is payable on services provided cross border vary according to the type of service involved and the status of the supplier and customer.

13.9.1. Basic rule

The basic rule for supplies to customers belonging outside the EU or to businesses within it is that the supply is treated as taking place where the customer belongs. This means where you supply services to a UK customer, VAT is due at the normal UK rates. If services are supplied to an EU business or any non-EU customer (business or not), no VAT is chargeable.

The basic rule doesn't apply where you supply services to a non-business customer in the EU. In this case you must charge VAT in the country where you belong. So assuming you're operating in the UK, you'll apply UK VAT rates.

EXAMPLE

Jack Jarrow is a personal tax consultant. He charges VAT to UK and EU clients but not to non-EU clients.

13.9.2. Exceptions to the basic rule

Whilst the basic rule applies to the majority of services, there are some exceptions.

Land. These transactions are taxed where the land is located. This includes:

- granting, assignment and surrender of leases and land options
- hotel and similar accommodation
- any works of construction, demolition, conversion, reconstruction, alteration, enlargement, repair or maintenance of a building or civil engineering work; and
- services supplied by estate agents, auctioneers, architects, surveyors.

Passenger transport. This is taxed where the transport takes place. Thus, UK VAT is due on UK transport, French VAT on transport in France etc. It will be necessary to apportion by reference to distance travelled where there is cross-border travel.

Cultural and artistic services, training and education. These are taxed in the state in which the performance venue is situated where they involve admission charges, e.g. tickets to a play or concert. Other services such as arranging events, training, conferences and the like that do not have an admission component are taxed under the basic rule.

Hire of means of transport. Short-term hire of cars, vans, planes and boats and ships are also subject to special rules.

In this context, short-term means up to 30 days unless the vehicle is a vessel in which case the limit is 90 days.

Short-term hire is taxed in the place where the vehicle is put at the customer's disposal. This is subject to use and enjoyment provisions.

EXAMPLE

Neil Newry runs a car hire business. He rents cars to businesses around his premises in Northern Ireland. He puts those cars at his customers' disposal in the UK for VAT purposes and so charges UK VAT. However, if he knows that his customers will use the cars for journeys across the border, he charges Irish VAT as the cars will be "used and enjoyed" in that other state.

Catering. This is taxed where it's provided.

Telecoms and hire of goods. These services are within the basic rule and taxed where the customer belongs but have a use and enjoyment test like the hire of means of transport.

There are two further areas of special treatment when the customer is a private individual in another EU state.

Goods transportation is taxed in the state within which the goods move, or if the goods cross an EU border, the state in which they began their journey. If the customer is a business, the basic rule applies.

Valuation services supplied to individuals in other states are taxed where the work is done.

13.9.3. The VAT reverse charge for services

A consequence of the above rules is that most supplies of services by UK businesses to EU business customers are VAT-free. This would be contrary to the basic concept of VAT that all supplies within the EU territory should be charged to VAT. The mechanism for ensuring that this basic rule is not broken is the so-called reverse charge.

Where you make a supply of a service to an EU business customer on which you don't have to charge VAT, the customer has to account for the VAT in their own country. Similarly, where your business buys services from a supplier in another EU country, you have to account for VAT on the purchase (in Box 1 of your VAT return) at UK VAT rates. You can then reclaim the VAT you've charged yourself subject to the normal claiming rules (Box 4 of your VAT return).

EXAMPLE

Jack Jarrow takes tax advice from a German accountant for a client and is charged £1,000. He calculates UK VAT at 20% and adds this into Box 1 of his VAT return as if it were UK output tax.

He is entitled to recover this VAT as input tax subject to the normal rules in Box 4. A partially exempt business may not be able to recover the input tax in Box 4.

Trap. If you're a non-registered UK customer, you must add the value of reverse charge services to your turnover to check whether you exceed the VAT registration limit. In other words, you can become liable to register in the UK because you purchase services from other businesses in the EU.

13.10. EU VAT SPECIAL CLAIM SYSTEM

One consequence of the special rules is that where a UK business incurs VAT in other member states on such things as hotels, meals, car hire and taxis, the foreign VAT can't be reclaimed through the UK VAT system. A special claim system exists for this purpose in all EU countries.

You can lodge an electronic claim through HMRC's website. The VATman vets the claim to ensure that you're entitled to make it and then forwards it to the authorities in the EU state in which the VAT was incurred. The authorities in that state then process the claim and repay the tax.

The form is relatively simple to complete and can usually be done entirely in English. It requires the business to sort the amounts claimed into cost categories and detail the expenses accordingly:

- fuel
- hiring of means of transport
- expenditure relating to means of transport
- road tolls and road user charge
- travel expenses, such as taxi fares, public transport fares
- accommodation
- food, drink and restaurant services
- admissions to fairs and exhibitions
- expenditure on luxuries, amusements and entertainment
- other.

Claims must be submitted within nine months of the calendar year in which the cost is incurred. All expenditure incurred in 2012 is eligible for claim until September 30 2013.

Claims for whole years must be for a minimum of €50. And where a claim is for less than a year, the minimum claim you can make is €400.

KEY POINTS

- exports of goods to businesses in other EU states are zero-rated
- exports to non-business customers in the EU must be charged to VAT as if they were being supplied to a UK customer
- exports to all non-EU customers can be zero-rated
- where you zero-rate, you must have proof that the goods were exported outside the UK within certain time limits
- where you import goods from within the EU you must supply your VAT number to make sure that the foreign business zero-rates the supply
- UK VAT is then charged by HMRC on imported goods; you can reclaim this VAT subject to the normal rules for input tax
- you can't reclaim foreign VAT charged on goods imported into the UK
- where you incur VAT on purchases in a foreign country, e.g. hotel accommodation, taxi fares, meals etc., you can reclaim this using the EU special claim system.

CHAPTER 14

VAT special situations

14.1. INTRODUCTION

There are many specialist rules within VAT law and practice which have developed over the life of the tax in the UK. Many of the provisions are designed to reflect particular commercial practices in certain trade sectors, facilitate ease of compliance or counter avoidance planning.

For other businesses the very nature of their trade means that the application of the VAT legislation to them is more complex than is normally the case, particularly those that are dealing in exempt services.

14.2. FINANCIAL SERVICES

If you operate in the financial sector, a wide range of the supplies you make will be exempt. And, as you can't reclaim VAT on purchases, where they relate to exempt supplies this can mean you'll have to bear the cost of this.

VAT exemption applies to the following services:

*   businesses providing credit - banks, loan companies, bureau de changes and any business that lends money (including inter-company loans within groups)
*   institutions operating bank and other types of savings and deposit accounts
*   stock brokers and others dealing in stocks and shares
*   pension funds and other investment funds dealing or investing in financial products
*   management services provided to most investment funds.

It also applies to brokers and other agents who arrange the supply of the exempt financial services listed above.

Trap. You may not consider yourself a broker of financial services but the rules can affect any business arranging finance, e.g. a shop providing HP contracts on its goods.

EXAMPLE

Our car dealer Barry Birmingham sells new cars. Not all of his customers can afford to pay the full purchase price but take out loans to cover the shortfall. Barry recommends Gordon Greenwich Finance as a source of funds, helps to complete the forms and proposes the loan to Gordon. For every loan that is taken out through Gordon, Barry receives a commission payment. This is exempt income for Barry.

Many businesses receive exempt income in the form of finance commissions and so need to consider whether there is a partial exemption input tax restriction to apply.

14.2.1. Offshore income tip

The financial sector exemption applies to income from UK and other EU sources. Income you receive from outside the EU is outside the scope of VAT. Contrary to the general rule which says that for the purposes of input VAT, "outside of the scope" supplies should be looked at as if they were being made in the UK, financial services will be treated as being equivalent to UK taxable income.

14.3. INSURANCE SERVICES

Insurance services are also subject to exemption, leaving those businesses with little or no input tax recovery.

The exemption applies to:

*   supplies of insurance and reinsurance
*   intermediary supplies by brokers and agents.

Trap. Insurance companies will have little input tax recovery available and insurance agents and brokers will also suffer high restrictions. Other businesses can also be affected by these provisions.

14.4. TOUR OPERATORS MARGIN SCHEME (TOMS)

The term tour operator can have a much wider reach than the name suggests. It covers any business which buys in travel services and sells them on to travellers as a package. The services covered under this scheme are generally passenger transport, accommodation excursions and guides.

Trap. While the rules are generally aimed at holiday companies putting together package tours, TOMS will apply to a business arranging a conference and organising transport and accommodation for delegates, or even a private school arranging a trip for its pupils.

The use of TOMS is mandatory where the supply you're making counts as that of a tour operator. The good news is that it gets around the tricky rules regarding the overseas element of VAT by treating all such supplies as subject to VAT in the country the supplier belongs; in other words, the UK for UK-based businesses. TOMS blocks you from reclaiming VAT on costs but means you only have to account for VAT on the gross margin, i.e. the profit element that you add on to the costs. The margin is based on the VAT-inclusive cost and so this gives a degree of input tax credit.

EXAMPLE

If you organise a business conference, say, in France, and invite delegates from within the industry to attend at a cost of £500 each, you'll only have to account for VAT on the margin you add over the direct costs. For example, where you paid a total of £400 including UK and overseas VAT for taxis, flights and hotel etc., you only have to account for VAT on the £100. The margin of £100 includes the VAT, so the amount you would have to pay to the VATman would be £16.67 (£100 x 20% / 120%).

The travel services designated as within TOMS are subject to standard-rated VAT for travel etc. within the EC and zero-rated if outside of it. Thus, if you only provide EC travel, the margin you make will be subject to VAT at 20%. If the travel is outside the EC, then there is no VAT to account for on the margin. Where there's a mix of EC and non-EC travel, the VAT chargeable on the margin is worked out in proportion to the costs you incur in relation to each element.

14.5. THE SUPPLY OF FOOD

The VAT treatment of supplies of food is renowned as being an area of great difficulty. Food is, in principle, zero-rated. However, there are many exceptions and complications that can even affect businesses outside the food industry.

VAT special situations

14

The first restriction is that food is not zero-rated where it is supplied in the course of catering. Catering is not defined in law but there is a clear suggestion that there's something else being provided, not just basic foodstuffs. This could be processing of food through to cooking it, serving food or providing dining facilities. A firm's canteen would certainly be caught by this rule and must standard-rate the food it supplies.

TIP

You can purchase food for consumption by your employees without having to bother about the VAT "catering" rules as long as generally you don't prepare, cook or process the food. But you can supply a microwave, toaster etc. for employees to do it themselves.

14.6. CHARITIES

It's a common misconception that charities are exempt from tax including VAT. While there are some reliefs available intended to apply only to charities, they are generally subject to the normal VAT rules. This means that any business activities will be subject to VAT in the same way as any other business.

Where you're making supplies of goods to a charity, you must charge VAT exactly as you would for any other customer. The one exception to this rule might be where you're selling them land or buildings, but it's up to the charity to make the running in terms of the special VAT treatment, so you don't have to worry about it.

Note. Where your business supplies advertising services to charities, this can be zero-rated.

14.7. SPORT

14.7.1. Letting of pitches and courts

Where your business includes the letting of facilities for the playing of sport, these are subject to the standard-rate VAT unless:

- it's for a continuous period in excess of 24 hours; or
- it's for a series of lets which are:
    - more than one but less than 14 days apart
    - for the same sport in the same location
    - paid for by reference to the whole series
    - providing exclusive use of the facility; and
    - provided to either a school, club or association or organisation representing clubs and associations.

In these situations you're making a supply of land which will usually be VAT exempt.

14.7.2. Eligible body supplies - members' clubs etc.

Non-profit making members clubs can exempt their supplies of sporting services to members under certain circumstances.

The exemption covers membership and playing fees along with other related services, such as locker hire. It doesn't extend to the supply of catering, accommodation or transport provided by a club.

Supplies will only be exempt where the body makes supplies to members who are defined as those persons being supplied with membership rights for a period of at least three months. Supplies made to guests of members aren't VAT exempt.

14.8. COMPETITION ENTRY FEES

Competition entry fees can be exempted where all of the income from such fees is returned by way of prizes.

14.9. CLOTHING AND PERSONAL PROTECTIVE EQUIPMENT

14.9.1. Clothing

Where your business sells clothing, this is generally standard-rated though there are some reliefs, most notably for children's clothing, which is zero-rated subject to the following conditions:

- **Design test.** The article of clothing must be designed with children in mind; this will mean that it is in a cut and style that are attractive to and suitable for children. It will also mean that the cut of the fabric takes into account the different body shapes of children when compared to adults. As a result of this, whilst there is no definition in law, the VATman states that he will not normally allow zero-rating for anything designed for someone over 13 years of age. The VATman lays down a series of measurements that they believe adequately define children's sizes. These vary from time to time.

- **Suitability test.** Rather harder to impose is the test that states that the article must not only be designed for young children but it must also not be suitable for older persons. In theory, this means that children's clothing will only qualify for relief if a petite adult who would fit into the item would not want to!

- **Fabric test.** There is generally no restriction on fabric. The only prohibition is the use of "fur skin" unless the item is headgear, gloves, buttons, belts or buckles. If the garment is not one of these, zero-rating is still possible as long as the fur is only a trimming and costs the manufacturer less than half of the total cost. For these purposes "fur skin" means any skin with fur, hair or wool attached except: **(1)** rabbit skin; **(2)** woolled sheep or lamb skin; or **(3)** the skin, if neither tanned nor dressed, of bovine cattle (including buffalo), equine animals, goats or kids (other than Yemen, Mongolian and Tibetan goats or kids), swine (including peccary), chamois, gazelles, deer or dogs.

This has to be the best definition in the whole of the VAT legislation. It appears to suggest that your child can have a zero-rated dog skin coat!

14.9.2. Protective boots and helmets

The sale of protective boots and helmets for industrial use can be also zero-rated (subject to being made in satisfaction of the various industrial standard kite mark tests).

Trap. The zero rate doesn't apply where you supply the goods to an employer for the use by its employees! Presumably the logic here is that the employer will be able to recover the VAT as input tax.

14.9.3. Motorcycle and pedal cycle helmets

The sale of helmets for use whilst riding motor and pedal cycles can be zero-rated where they meet the relevant kite standards.

14.10. REVERSE CHARGE GOODS TRAP

There are some industries where there has been significant abuse of the VAT system and this has led to special rules in the form of reverse charge accounting in certain circumstances. These rules apply to businesses that supply mobile communication devices and computer chips for business customers, and where the invoice value exceeds £5,000.

No VAT should be charged where you supply these goods; instead, your customer must account for it as if it were their own output tax on their VAT return. On the same return they are entitled to recover it as input tax, subject to the normal rules.

KEY POINTS

- the sale of financial products, e.g. insurance, even as a broker, is VAT exempt. This can mean your right to recover input tax in full is restricted under the partial exemption rules
- the Tour Operators Margin Scheme (TOMS) applies to any business that organises travel arrangements for others, e.g. a company which arranges and sells places on a business seminar including transport or accommodation
- the supply of food is zero-rated unless it's in the course of catering. Firms' canteens must standard-rate their food
- charities are not exempt from VAT and must charge it at the normal rates where they are carrying on a business activity
- not-for-profit members' clubs are exempt and so do not have to charge VAT on fees. The exemption doesn't apply to guests attending the club
- the sale of children's clothing can be zero-rated
- no VAT is chargeable on the sale of certain electronic goods to other businesses, e.g. mobile phones and computer chips.

VAT special situations

CHAPTER 15

Appendices

Appendix 1

SUPPLIES THAT DON'T COUNT FOR REGISTRATION PURPOSES

All exempt supplies ignore the VAT registration turnover test. The most common types of supply falling into this category are:

- finance - dealing in money, credit facilities, including loans
- land - rents, freehold, and leasehold sales of a major interest (see Appendix 6 for more details)
- charity fundraising events
- education services
- health services by doctors, dentists, opticians, nurses etc.
- cultural services - museum entrance fees, and music or theatre put on by public bodies
- sports competitions and physical education
- insurance and directly linked services
- betting and gaming
- antiques - sales from historic homes
- burial etc. services
- investment gold
- subscriptions to trade bodies, e.g. a trade union or professional association.

Supplies outside the scope of VAT also do not count as turnover.

Any supplies which would be exempt from VAT or outside the scope of the tax are to be left out. The result of this is that some very substantial businesses have no requirement to be VAT registered as their taxable supplies are low in value and they derive their income from exempt or other sources.

Appendix 2

FLAT RATE SCHEME PERCENTAGES

BUSINESS CATEGORY	PERCENTAGE APPLICABLE
Accountancy or bookkeeping	13
Advertising	10
Agricultural services	10
Any other activity not listed elsewhere	10.5
Architect, civil and structural engineer or surveyor	13
Boarding or care of animals	10.5
Business services that are not listed elsewhere	10.5
Catering services including restaurants and takeaways	11
Computer and IT consultancy or data processing	13
Computer repair services	9.5
Dealing in waste or scrap	9.5
Entertainment or journalism	11
Estate agency or property management services	10.5
Farming or agriculture that is not listed elsewhere	6
Film, radio, television or video production	11.5
Financial services	12
Forestry or fishing	9.5
General building or construction services*	8.5
Hairdressing or other beauty treatment services	11.5
Hiring or renting goods	8.5
Hotel or accommodation	9.5
Investigation or security	10.5
Labour-only building or construction services*	13
Laundry or dry-cleaning services	10.5
Lawyer or legal services	13
Library, archive, museum or other cultural activity	8.5
Management consultancy	12.5
Manufacturing that is not listed elsewhere	8.5
Manufacturing fabricated metal products	9.5
Manufacturing food	8
Manufacturing yarn, textiles or clothing	8
Membership organisation	7

15

Appendices

BUSINESS CATEGORY	PERCENTAGE APPLICABLE
Mining or quarrying	9
Packaging	8
Photography	10
Post offices	4.5
Printing	7.5
Publishing	10
Pubs	6
Real estate activity not listed elsewhere	12.5
Repairing personal or household goods	9
Repairing vehicles	7.5
Retailing food, confectionary, tobacco, newspapers or children's clothing	3.5
Retailing pharmaceuticals, medical goods, cosmetics or toiletries	7
Retailing that is not listed elsewhere	6.5
Retailing vehicles or fuel	6
Secretarial services	11.5
Social work	10
Sport or recreation	7.5
Transport or storage, including couriers, freight, removals and taxis	9
Travel agency	9.5
Veterinary medicine	10
Wholesaling agricultural products	7
Wholesaling food	6.5
Wholesaling that is not listed elsewhere	7.5

* *"Labour-only building or construction services" relates to building or construction services where the value of materials supplied is less than 10% of turnover from such services.*

Other building or construction services are covered by rate applying to "General building or construction".

Appendix 3

APPEALING AGAINST A REQUEST FOR A VAT SECURITY PAYMENT

If you disagree with the VATman's decision that you should make a security payment, you have the right to an independent review of that decision. You should put your request in writing to the VAT office which issued the security demand. You must request a review within 30 days of the date of issue of the Notice of Requirement to give security.

Common reasons for asking for a review include that you believe:

- all the facts may not have been properly considered, if at all

- you can provide further information that would influence the VATman's decision.

Where after a statutory review the VATman still demands a security payment, you can appeal to the tax tribunal to consider the matter, although you can if you wish skip the review procedure and make an appeal direct to the tribunal.

An application for a tribunal hearing can be downloaded from the Tribunals Service website: http://www.tribunals.gov.uk/tax/Documents/NoticeofAppeal_Jun10.pdf

Appendix 4

APPEALING AGAINST A VAT PENALTY OR SURCHARGE

VAT surcharges

If you disagree with the VATman's surcharge, you can dispute it in one of two ways:

- ask to have your case reviewed by an officer not previously involved in your case
- have your case heard by the tax tribunal.

If you want a review, you must write to the following address within 30 days of the date the surcharge liability notice extension was sent to you, giving the reasons why you disagree with the decision.

Surcharge Appeals
Crownhill Court
Tailyour Road
Crownhill
Plymouth
PL6 5BZ

Where you opt for a review by the VATman, you still have the right to appeal to the tax tribunal if you disagree with his decision.

VAT penalties

The procedure for appealing against any VAT penalty is similar to that for VAT surcharge described above. However, your request for an internal review should be sent to the VAT office which issued the penalty notice. Alternatively, you could appeal to the tax tribunal straight away. In this case you'll need to send a completed application to the tribunal within 30 days of the issue of the penalty notice. An application can be downloaded from http://www.tribunals.gov.uk/tax/Documents/NoticeofAppeal_Jun10.pdf

Appendix 5

REGISTRATION THRESHOLDS

Austria	All businesses: Nil
Belgium	Non-resident businesses: Nil
Bulgaria	Non-resident: 50,000 BGN
Cyprus	Non-resident: Euro 15,600
Czechoslovakia	Non-resident businesses: Nil
Denmark	Non-resident: 50,000 BGN
Estonia	Non-resident: Nil
Finland	Non-resident: Nil
France VAT Rate	Non-resident: Nil
Germany	Non-resident: Nil
Greece	Non-resident: Nil
Hungary	Non-resident: Nil
Ireland (Eire)	Non-resident: Nil
Italy	Non-resident: Nil
Latvia	Non-resident: Nil
Lithuania	Non-resident: Nil
Luxembourg	Non-resident: Nil
Malta	Non-resident: Nil
Netherlands	Non-resident: Nil
Poland	Non-resident: Nil
Portugal	Non-resident: Nil
Romania	Non-resident: Nil
Slovakia	Non-resident: Nil
Slovenia	Non-resident: Nil
Spain	Non-resident: Nil
Sweden	Non-resident: Nil
Norway	Non-resident: 50,000 NOK
Switzerland	Non-resident: CHF 100,000

Appendix 6

LAND AND BUILDINGS

Introduction

Dealing in land and buildings is arguably the most complicated VAT area. Depending on the exact circumstances, supplies could be standard-rated, reduced-rated, zero-rated, exempt or even outside the scope of the tax altogether. Knowing the different rules is vital in ensuring that you don't pay too much or reclaim too little VAT. And as land and buildings tend be high value items, getting it wrong can be very expensive.

Why is it important to establish the correct VAT treatment?

Whether you're developing, converting or selling a property, you'll incur expenses which include VAT. Where you sell or transfer the property and charge VAT at the zero or standard rate, you'll be able to reclaim the VAT on your costs but not where the sale or transfer is exempt.

VAT and residential property

There are two types of transaction involving residential property to which zero-rating applies: one for the sale, and one for carrying out work.

Sale

To quote the VAT rules directly, zero-rating applies to, *"The first grant of a major interest in a building or part of a building designed as a dwelling or number of dwellings by a person constructing it"*.

- **Grant of a major interest.** This means the disposal (sale or other transfer) of a freehold property, or the grant of a lease lasting more than 21 years (at least 20 if you are in Scotland).

  Note. The grant of a shorter lease is exempt, as are second and subsequent grants.

  For example, where a business grants 75-year leases on new flats it has constructed, they would be zero-rated. But where the leaseholder sells the lease, it will be exempt. Similarly, if the same business instead granted leases of less than 21 years, these would be exempt, but where it later sells the freehold of the property, or grants a head-lease of more than 21 years, these transactions would be zero-rated because they would be the "first grant of a major interest", i.e. the original short leases don't count as major interests.

- **Dwelling.** The term "dwelling" here takes on its normal meaning but in particular we are looking for sufficient living accommodation to occupy as a home which is self-contained, has no direct internal access to another dwelling, is subject to no restriction on separate use or disposal and has been constructed in line with any required planning consent which has been obtained. Thus, putting a granny annex next to your house will not qualify for relief if it has a door through to the house.

- **Person constructing.** There has to be construction of a new dwelling for zero-rating to apply. This could be a new build on bare land, or following demolition of existing buildings or extension of those old buildings either upwards or sideways. The person constructing will be the developer or contractor actually carrying out the work.

There could be more than one person constructing. A developer could sell a part-completed house to another developer. As long as the house has progressed beyond foundations (the so-called "golden brick" stage) this is zero-rated. The second builder completes the house and sells it. This too is a zero-rated sale.

Constructing in this context generally means that a building is being built from the ground up. It's possible to retain some parts of a previous dwelling and still qualify for zero-rating but the rules are tightly drawn and have been at the centre of many VAT cases heard by the courts.

Examples of new-builds that count as zero-rated are:

- building against a flank wall of another house such as the end of a terrace
- building between two flank walls, such as infilling in the middle of a terrace
- building on a corner site
- using one existing wall following demolition of a previous residential building as long as this is a condition of the planning permission.

> ### TIP
>
> The courts have ruled on a number of occasions that an existing free-standing skeleton for a building, such as a steel or wooden frame, does not constitute an existing building. So, for example, if you're constructing an office from an old barn which is stripped down to the bare frame, the reconstruction will be zero-rated rather than exempt. This means you can recover the VAT on your costs.

Where you're building on an existing frame or replacing a demolished building, take pictures of the original structure and after demolition. This will serve as evidence should the VATman challenge the zero-rating.

Selling buildings for charitable or residential use

The disposal zero-rating also applies to other major interest grants if the buildings are either to be used for a relevant residential purpose (RRP) or a relevant charitable purpose (RCP).

What counts as an RRP?

A RRP broadly speaking is a communal dwelling for use as:

- a home or other institution providing residential accommodation for children

- a home or other institution providing residential accommodation with personal care for persons in need of such care by reason of old age, disability, dependence on alcohol or drugs (whether past or present) or mental disorder (whether past or present)

- a hospice

- residential accommodation for students or school pupils

- residential accommodation for members of any of the armed forces

- a monastery, nunnery, or similar establishment

- an institution which is the sole or main residence of at least 90% of its residents.

What counts as an RCP?

A RCP is to be used:

- for non-business charitable purposes (other than an office); or

- a village hall or similar building.

Note. The VATman allows up to 5% business use of an RCP before he will argue that the zero-rating will not apply.

Zero-rated sale of a converted building

The zero-rating of a first grant extends to dwellings created through conversion, but not in every case. The building being converted must be one that was neither designed or adapted as a dwelling, number of dwellings or as a RRP building, or if was so designed or adapted, has not been used for such purposes for at least ten years.

As a result, converting commercial buildings such as offices, warehouses, barns etc. to residential use will result in the sale being zero-rated. This means you can reclaim VAT on the costs of conversion.

Zero-rated construction

The second part of the zero-rating regime applies to supplies made in the course of construction of a zero-rated dwelling. The idea is that the owner/developer should not have to pay VAT on having work done on constructing a building which they will sell a zero-rated interest in. It would be a waste of everyone's time and effort if the owner/developer just reclaims the VAT back but has to temporarily fund the cost of it until then.

What counts as zero-rated construction work?

This covers all works of construction for new dwellings, RRP and RCP buildings and conversions carried out for a Housing Association.

Note. Zero-rating does not apply to work on buildings being converted to dwellings either from commercial use or under the ten-year non-residential use rule. These will be subject to the reduced rate (see below).

The zero-rating will apply to all businesses supplying the services whether as main or sub-contractors for most constructions but only main contractors for RRP and RCP buildings.

Trap. The services of professionals such as architects, project managers, surveyors and the like are excluded from zero-rating and so will be standard-rated.

TIP

Building materials supplied by contractors who are also supplying zero-rated construction services can also be zero-rated.

Trap. Where the contractor supplies other goods, e.g. kitchen appliances such as cookers and fridges, the VAT rules say they can't zero-rate the supply of these and you can't recover the VAT they charge. There's a specific block on input tax recovery for all items which do not qualify as ordinary fixtures and fittings. This will mean different things in different buildings. What is normally installed in a church may be different to that for a house.

The VATman often argues that landscaping work does not qualify as construction services and so does not benefit from zero-rating.

TIP

If the planting scheme and work are included in the planning application and so become part of the planning permission, the VATman will usually accept relief.

Zero-rating and protected buildings

The zero-rating applies in two ways to listed (protected) buildings

- sale; and
- reparation works.

Sale

The zero-rating applies to the first grant of a major interest in a dwelling in a protected building by a person substantially reconstructing it. Substantial reconstruction in this situation means that:

- the building is being reconstructed
- at least 60% of the works were approved alterations and only incorporates external walls and features of architectural or historic interest.

Trap. Where any internal features are retained, the zero-rating doesn't apply.

Approved alterations

The second part of the zero-rating covers works in the course of carrying out approved alterations to protected buildings.

Trap. Again, professional fees are specifically excluded from the zero-rating.

Approved alterations are those works to a protected building which:

- require listed buildings council consent; and
- alter the fabric of the building in a meaningful way.

Zero-rating of approved alterations is less important for businesses which occupy a listed building, as unless they are exempt or partially exempt they will be able to reclaim the full amount of VAT charged by the builder carrying out the work. But for unregistered businesses, those which make some or all exempt supplies, or private individuals, they will not be able to reclaim some or all of the VAT. And so it's vital that they make sure that the builder carrying out the work zero-rates the charges.

Reduced-rate VAT on buildings

The reduced VAT rate of 5% applies to a range of services but never to the sale of a property.

Conversions

There are three designated types of conversion which qualify for the reduced rate.

1. Changed number of dwellings conversion. As the name suggests, the main requirement is that, after conversion, the building being converted contains at least one dwelling and it had a different number of dwellings before work commenced. The result is that conversion of a dwelling can qualify for reduced rating as long as the number of dwellings changes as a result of the work. This will mainly affect those converting commercial to residential, splitting large houses into flats or vice versa, i.e. turning flats into fewer flats or even a single dwelling.

EXAMPLE

Boris Bolton purchases a derelict pub. He converts the ground floor public area into two flats. The upper parts used to be a staff flat. He refurbishes this flat. The conversion of the pub qualifies for the reduced rate. There was no dwelling there originally and now there are two. Refurbishing the flat does not qualify under this heading as the number of dwellings has not changed. This means that Boris can ask the builder carrying out the work to charge him VAT at the lower rate.

TIP

Boris should purchase the fixtures and fittings, e.g. sinks, taps, door furniture etc. for the dwelling through his builder rather than directly. The builder can pass them on to Boris and charge only 5% VAT, whereas if he bought the fittings etc. direct from the shops, he will have to pay standard-rate (20%) VAT. Once again, the professional services relating to the conversion, e.g. architects' fees, are excluded from the lower rate VAT charge. Boris will have to pay full VAT on these.

© TRIED AND TESTED WAYS TO REDUCE YOUR VAT BILL, INDICATOR

If Boris were to sell or grant a long lease (more than 21 years) over the converted buildings, the sale is zero-rated, and the reduced-rate VAT he paid can be reclaimed.

2. Special residential conversion. The lower VAT rate applies to a conversion where a building that's not used for RRP is converted into a building that can be.

   Trap. One key requirement that is often overlooked is that the services only qualify for relief under this heading if they are supplied to a person who will use the property for those relevant purposes. If they are provided to anyone else, they will be standard-rated. That means the VAT break is only of use to nursing homes and the like.

3. Residential renovations and alterations. The reduced rate also applies to renovation and alteration work on residential property which has not been used as such for at least two years at the commencement of the work. In our example above, Boris bought a derelict pub. If the flat above the pub had not been occupied for at least two years, the renovation work on it would qualify for reduced rating under this heading.

VAT on commercial property

VAT rules say that sales/disposals and letting of property are exempt. This includes sales of freeholds, leases, lease surrenders, reverse surrenders and assignments. Some sales etc. of commercial buildings and structures and other rights over land are excluded from the exemption and so are subject to standard-rate VAT:

- the freehold disposal of new or part-completed non-residential buildings. In this context a building is new for a period of three years from the earlier of completion (architects issue of certificate of practical completion) or first full occupation
- the right to take game or fish unless the grant is that of the freehold
- sleeping and catering accommodation in hotels, inns, boarding houses or similar establishments
- holiday accommodation
- seasonal caravan pitches
- tent pitches and camping facilities
- vehicle parking
- the right to fell and remove standing timber
- housing and storage of aircraft, or mooring of ships and boats
- the right to occupy a seat or box at a sports ground, theatre, concert hall etc.

- sporting rights unless:
- there is a grant for a continuous period of 24 hours or more or a series of at least ten lets
- each let is for the same sport at the same venue
- the interval between the lets is more than one day but not more than 14
- consideration is payable by reference to the whole series
- there is exclusive use of the facility; and
- the grantee is a school, club or association or organisation representing a club or association.

Opting to charge VAT on exempt buildings

The general exemption for commercial property can be a problem for businesses and other organisations. Consider someone wanting to start a commercial property investment business. Where it purchases a new building, i.e. one that's less than three years old, this will be excluded from the exemption, meaning VAT at the standard rate will be charged by the developer. This is a real cost to the business as when it rents out the property it too will be making exempt supplies, i.e. rent, meaning that as an exempt business it won't be entitled to claim any VAT on purchases, large or small. But the good news is that there is a way around this problem; it can waive the exemption on the property - this is called making an "option to tax". By doing so it will have to charge VAT on the rent to its tenants but it means it can reclaim the VAT it pays on the cost of the building.

Generally speaking, the option to tax will be useful to businesses that intend to rent out the building, but there are other situations where it's a good thing, e.g. when acquiring a property as part of going concern (see below).

Residential use buildings

Even where you opt to tax a building it will not have any effect if it will be used for residential purposes. But where a building contains both residential and non-residential parts, the option can be made but will be only effective on the non-residential parts.

EXAMPLE

Boris Bolton has renovated his pub keeping the ground floor as a commercial operation - as a bar - while upstairs is a residential apartment. It costs him a great deal for the conversion but if he were to sell the property it would be exempt and so all the VAT paid for the renovation would be irrecoverable. But if he opts to tax the building and charges VAT on the sale, he would be able to reclaim the VAT on the renovation work. The option only has effect on the ground floor bar; it does not affect the flat above which is residential and so proceeds of the sale relating to this are VAT exempt.

Intended conversion to residential use

If a building is subject to an option to tax, the purchaser can make it ineffective where they declare to the vendor that their intention is to use the property for residential use. They can do this by providing a certificate (Form VAT1614D) to the vendor.

This issue of the certificate of residential use has to be given before a price is agreed to allow the vendor to negotiate a value taking into account any of the VAT he reclaimed on purchase of the property that he may have to pay back to the VATman under the partial exemption or capital goods scheme rules.

What can an option to tax apply to?

An option can be made in respect of land or buildings.

If the option is taken on land, it covers all items attached to that land, including buildings either already on the land or constructed at a later date.

It the option is taken in respect of buildings, it is effective in relation to the buildings and also the land on which it stands whether the building remains or not.

Where a new building is constructed on opted land, the option automatically applies to that building. This could be inconvenient where you would prefer to rent out a property on an exempt basis.

TIP

The option to tax can be overridden in these circumstances; a new commercial property can be taken out of the scope of the option by sending a Form VAT1614F to HMRC before the earlier of:

- the grant of an interest in the building is made

- occupation of the building; and

- completion of the construction (this is usually accepted as being the time at which the architect issues a certificate of completion).

Trap. Submitting Form VAT1614F is allowed at any time after construction has progressed beyond foundation level. But from that date, as the building will then be exempt from VAT it means no input tax VAT on the build costs can be reclaimed.

Can parts of a building be subject to an option to tax?

Where an option is taken in respect of a building, it will apply to the whole building even where the person or business opting only has an interest in part of the building. In other words, it's not possible to opt to tax only part of a building. Not only that but the option will apply to all other buildings linked with it internally or by covered walkways. It will also affect all buildings in complex units that are part of the same enclosed concourse.

Considerations before opting

Input tax

The only significant benefit of opting is the recovery of input tax. Therefore, the option should only be exercised where the input tax gain is worthwhile.

Tenants and purchasers

Opting will mean that VAT will be due on rental and sale proceeds of the property unless it's to be used for residential purposes. If the tenants or purchasers can't reclaim the VAT, it will make the property more expensive for them and so a less attractive proposition to buy or rent, meaning you might have to reduce your price or rent.

Revoking an option

Once an option has been taken, it generally applies for 20 years. Before opting to tax you need to consider whether this long-term arrangement is likely to suit you. For example, you might want to rent it out to an exempt or partly exempt business in future. If so, they won't be able to recover the VAT.

Notifying the VATman of an option

Once you've decided to opt, you must notify the VATman using Form VAT1614A or in a letter containing all the information shown on the form. This should be done within 30 days.

Personal nature of option

Where you dispose of your interest in a property on which you've made an election, the option still applies to you after the sale; it does not pass to the purchaser.

The only time an option by one business applies automatically to others is where the business is a member of a VAT group. An option taken by one member of a VAT group is treated as being taken by all of the current members and businesses joining the group at a later date.

The effect of options on mixed developments

Where a building development has mixed exempt and taxable use, it's necessary to apportion the cost between them.

EXAMPLE

Boris Bolton purchases a row of shops. The shops have offices above. Boris intends to refurbish the shops and let them. He opts to tax in order to recover associated input tax. He is going to convert the offices into flats and also build a whole new floor comprised of new flats.

The shop refurbishment is standard-rated, the conversion work reduced-rated and the new-build residential zero-rated. His builder will charge him £240,000. They analyse the costings and agree that 25% will be standard-rated, 35% subject to 5% VAT and the balance will be zero-rated.

Trap. VAT law says that an apportionment of this nature may be made but it's not required. If no apportionment is made, the VATman believes that the whole contract sum is liable to the standard rate. This could be very expensive if the customer were to make exempt supplies.

Notes

Notes

Notes

Notes

Notes

Notes

Notes

Notes

Notes

Notes

Notes